Mindset
Matters

Scripture quotations taken from The Holy Bible, New International Version® NIV® (unless otherwise noted) Copyright © 1973 1978 1984 2011 by Biblica, Inc. TM Used by permission. All rights reserved worldwide.

Copyright © 2020 by Matthew Hunt

All rights reserved. No part of this publication may be reproduced, distributed, or transmitted in any form or by any means, including photocopying, recording, or other electronic or mechanical methods, without the prior written permission of the author, except in the case of brief quotations embodied in critical reviews and certain other noncommercial uses permitted by copyright law.

Printed in the United States
ISBN# 978-1-945121-13-5

www.swiftwordpublishing.com

Mindset
Matters

SETTING YOUR THOUGHTS TOWARDS
A GOD-HONORING PERSPECTIVE

by Matthew Hunt

ACKNOWLEDGMENTS

I love my Faith Church friends and family. This book represents the deepest values we hold onto as a congregation. Our mindset matters because it shapes our purpose and filters our priorities. This book is for our church, but I believe the message resonates with others too.

The seven mindsets discussed in these pages are our story. They articulate a glimpse into our feeble attempts to represent the real Jesus as a community. These are our mindsets, and it matters deeply to us.

I am truly honored to serve among people willing to walk-out genuine faith, live in a way that shifts the culture, and passionate about bringing heaven to our part of the earth. The mission God has us on is humbling. We are not a perfect church, and we're okay with that reality.

I am genuinely grateful to my editor, Carole, whose hard work truly helped me write better. Also, a big thank you to my friend, Clayton, who helped get this project started and across the finish line.

May God continue to be present in our lives as we set our minds in alignment with God's best. I hope we never stop honoring God first and creating a community where others experience a sense of belonging. I pray we always remember our Mindset Matters!

FAITH CHURCH MANIFESTO

At Faith Church, we are bringing faith to life. We are committed to fulfilling Jesus' mission to love God and love others – it's faith put to action. We want to connect faith to life in the city of Fort Scott and in every surrounding town. Jesus is the center of our focus, and we want to live out our faith in every endeavor, conversation, and each place we go. We strive toward generosity and gratitude as we desire to be spirit-led in everything. We choose a faith that is committed rather than casual, so we always contribute more than we consume. We are faith-filled in the pursuit of our mission, allowing God's Word to shape our worldview and priorities. We choose to focus on a few priorities, making them excellent instead of becoming distracted by many good things. Our priorities are: creating life-giving services, partnering in outreach both globally and locally, engaging in life-building connect groups, and creating irresistible kids environments at every level. We believe unity releases God's blessing, so we remain humble in our choice to give honor to others. No matter if you are far from faith, familiar with faith in Jesus, or have just fallen away – you belong here. Welcome to the faith journey; we believe you'll find life.

www.faithchurchks.org

Table of Contents

[1] Mindset *Matters*   8

[2] The Center   14

[3] Make Room   37

[4] Committed Contributor   56

[5] Focus   75

[6] Unity with Humility   96

[7] Expectation + Gratitude   119

[8] Generosity + Stewardship   139

[9] Final Thoughts   159

Endnotes   166

[1] Mindset *Matters*

I'm a big fan of GPS. GPS is a lifeline for me. In fact, if it weren't for my GPS on my phone, I probably would need to be in a support group for anger management! I have zero confidence in my sense of direction. I have three beautiful kids; my manhood doesn't hinge on being good with directions. HA!

My wife, on the other hand, is incredible with directions and she's the best navigator I know. She can go somewhere one time, and she photographically remembers how to get there a second time. She is so good that sometimes Siri asks my wife for directions!

One thing I find interesting about a GPS is that a GPS will tell you exactly where you are, but it can't tell you where you're going. It cannot tell you how to get to a specific place until you input some coordinates. Your GPS is fantastic at revealing where you are right now. But if you don't input an address or the destination you want to go, the GPS can't help you at all.

A GPS is designed to direct you to a predetermined destination. It only works when you know where you want to go.

The same is true in your life. You cannot accidentally get to your destination or desired outcome. Never in one's life has anyone awakened and said, "Oh hey look, I bought my dream house. What a surprise!"

No, if you want to arrive at a specific place in your life or achieve something, it will not happen by accident. It requires some intentional input on your part. You must add the proper data to help you arrive at your life's destiny.

Your mindset reveals a lot about your current position and your future potential. Your mindset is like your GPS. The thoughts you input will determine your destination. Your pattern of thinking will direct you to a destination. Your mindset really does matter.

So, the question becomes, "Do you like the direction your thoughts are taking you?"

You will not wake up one day to discover you are accidentally financially secure, have a thriving marriage, or are serving God with your whole heart.

Accomplishing these things takes some intentionality. Living out your destiny and dreams requires you to input the proper data in your mindset. The context of your life is set entirely by what you embed into your mind.

What you think about day in and day out will determine where you end up in your life. For example, by choosing to think differently about your spouse, you can change what you experience in your house.

Your attention determines your destination. Your eyes and thoughts are attracting you toward something.

I remember learning how to drive. I was timid but focused. I regularly watched both sides of the road to ensure that I stayed between the lines. The idea of drifting into the ditch or into the other lane scared me straight. The problem was that I kept swerving within my lane, causing the ride to be anything but smooth.

It wasn't until I learned to set my sights on what's ahead, instead of looking at the ditches on either side, that things started to ride a little more smoothly.

Similarly, life stays on course when we set our sights where we want to go, instead of on where we are now or where we have been in the past. If we're going to avoid the drift, we must set our sights ahead.

When we begin to set our minds in agreement with God's purposes and plans, we begin to navigate toward the destiny He has for us. We find ourselves living an abundant and satisfying life full of meaning!

That is my hope for you. I want to see you living out the dream and destiny God has for you. I want your marriage to be full of passion. I want to see your finances flourish.

When we begin to **set our minds** in agreement **with God's purposes and plans,** we begin to navigate toward the destiny He has for us.

#MindsetMattersBook

I want you to live from a place of purpose, finding satisfaction. I want you to experience the good plans God has for your life. "For I know the plans I have for you," declares the Lord, "plans to prosper you and not to harm you, plans to give you hope and a future." (Jer. 29:11)
Even though the Lord has good plans for us, remember, we don't accidentally arrive there. We must set our minds on that destination.

My desire for this book is to help you set your mind on things that matter. I want to help you chart a course toward a spiritually satisfying life – finding God's abundance in everything.

This book will explore seven mindsets that have made a difference for me and are central to our church. These mindsets set us on a course to find God's best!

[2] The Center

As a kid, I participated in a Christian version of the Boy Scouts. It was called Royal Rangers. Royal Rangers came complete with a motto, pledges, badges, and an embarrassing mandatory wardrobe. As soon as I was old enough to opt-out, I did. It was not my jam.

However, one good thing I recall being taught in Royal Rangers was how to use a compass. I remember two key facts; the compass helps you know the direction you're pointing, and it operates magnetically. A magnet is what makes a compass point north – the pin is a small magnet that is suspended so that it can spin freely inside its casing, responding to our planet's magnetic pull.[1]

Life is too important to live without a sense of direction. Our mindsets help us to navigate life well. But just like we need a compass in the wilderness, we need a centering point that draws us toward our destiny. We need a compass to navigate the twists and turns through life.

Life is too **important** to live without a sense of **direction.**

#MindsetMattersBook

KEEP JESUS AT THE CENTER

Everything in our life should center on Jesus. He should be the source code, powering our actions. Jesus is the magnet drawing us toward our true north – our destiny. If we don't fix our mindset on Jesus, we can easily drift off-center in our lives.

At our church, we want Jesus to be the focal point of any activity we endeavor to do. He is the main celebrity of all the stuff, all the praise, all the glory – everything points to Jesus.

With Jesus at the center, we want His Word – the Bible, the Holy Scriptures, that collection of writings – as our compass. We believe that the Bible is inerrant, that it is 100 percent written by man under the inspiration of the Holy Spirit.

"All Scripture is God-breathed and is useful for teaching, rebuking, correcting and training in righteousness," (2 Tim. 3:16)

Every word of the Bible has the life of God breathed into it, and His Spirit is air-locked within these words. Every time you flip one of those pages, the life of God is released a little more into you as you are reading.

I have found that the Bible reads me as I read it. It helps me discover who I am and where I'm going. I find course corrections for my journey, instructions or training for my leadership and parenting, and I find inspiration to keep moving toward Jesus.

Every single book in the Bible points to Jesus. In fact, the entire book is really all about Him. When we remove Jesus from the center, we lose our true north. We need Jesus so we can see God the Father correctly.

Jesus said it this way, "Anyone who has seen me has seen the Father. "(Jn. 14:9) In other words, if we've lost our way to God, we must first start looking for Jesus in order to find our way back.

#FORYOU

I've always been drawn to the world of marketing and branding, probably because it combines two things I enjoy – creativity and communication. A central component to being successful in the marketplace is to remain on brand with your messaging. You don't want to create an ad campaign that is inconsistent with your company's mission.

The images, colors, messaging, and even the personality of the writings must reinforce the mission of the company. If you change even one of these on-brand elements, perhaps trying to be a little clever sounding, you may accidentally make your message less clear. Sure, you might get people's attention, but it likely won't be very helpful.

I recently read an article about mistakes people make when marketing. One example was from Coca-Cola. When Coke first started to market using their name in China, it was sometimes translated as "Bite the Wax Tadpole." I am sure that created some curiosity but was probably not very helpful in selling their beverage!

In the same article, I also read about a company called Powergen Italia and how they wanted to expand into English-speaking countries. They decided to go with the most obvious website address – www.powergenitalia.com.[2] Whoops! Not the best idea and certainly wasn't going to help them reach their intended market!

The church, too, can suffer from these same kinds of mistakes. When we allow our mindset to be shaped by anything other than Jesus, we create brand confusion. We begin looking for ways to tighten our circles and keep others on the outside. We create confusion in our messaging as representatives of Christ. For example, we might try to sound clever by posting some internet "meme" that seems to relate to our faith, but we might be accidentally confusing the point. A meme may claim to be telling the "truth", but we must ask ourselves, is it helpful to share this?

As a church, we started using the hashtag #ForYou. We chose this because we wanted our message to be clear - the message that God is FOR you, not against you, and so are we! We believe #ForYou represents the heart of God and centers on His love, not your behavior. Too many people live with a false mindset that God is mad and waiting to strike them down. We don't believe that's "on-brand" for Christians.

No, I'm not trying to reduce the Son of God to a brand. I don't believe following Jesus is just a "brand" of living; I am convinced that Jesus IS life. But we want to accurately represent Him. We don't want to resemble a broken compass!

Our mindset matters. It must be shaped by Jesus. He needs to be the magnet at the center of every decision, every ideology, every thought, every sermon, every worship song, and every investment we make. If the day ever comes that we are not drawing closer to Him personally, or have stopped bringing others closer to Him, then He is no longer at the center.

KEEP IMAGINING

I love the power of story. There is something transcendent and motivating about an inspiring story. One classic example is the children's literary series by C.S. Lewis, *The Chronicles of Narnia*. *The Chronicles of Narnia* has a way of inspiring our imaginations to see an alternate world behind a magic wardrobe, complete with talking creatures we can interact with and from whom we can learn valuable truths.

God's Word is similar in its ability to inspire. It is full of stories that excite our imaginations. The truths that

> "Your **imagination** is the **incubator** of your faith.

#MindsetMattersBook

are hidden in those real-life stories help us to grasp very important truths.

Your imagination is the incubator of your faith. We read in Hebrews 11:1, "Now faith is confidence in what we hope for and assurance about what we do not see." What is Hope? Hope is the picture, or image, in our mind's eye of a desired outcome. Whenever someone loses hope, they often say something like, "I just don't see it anymore." They lose faith because they lost the picture in their minds of what could be.

Reading the stories in Scripture feeds our hope and encourages our faith to grow. The stories of the Bible help us imagine God's faithfulness, His mercy, His protection, His guidance, and His love.

This is the reason that in our ministry environments for kids up to fifth grade, we focus so much on stories in the Bible. If we can inspire a child's imagination to see what God has done, then it helps them to believe what God can do! We want to put Jesus on their level. We want to craft experiences for our kids that inspire their imagination and activate their faith.

FIX YOUR EYES

What does it look like to live a life where Jesus is the center of your focus and His Word is your compass? What does that mean on Monday morning, when the 5 a.m. alarm clock starts the week? How does Jesus live at the center of your daily life during the work week? How does Jesus live at the center of a life on the weekend when everybody around you wants to go get drunk? How do you live with God's Word as your compass in a family where everybody else seems to be anti-God?

Let's look at a scripture.

> *"Therefore, since we are surrounded by such a great cloud of witnesses, let us throw off everything that hinders and the sin that so easily entangles. And let us run with perseverance the race marked out for us, fixing our eyes on Jesus, the pioneer, and perfecter of faith. For the joy set before him, he endured the cross, scorning its shame, and sat down at the right hand of the throne of God. Consider him who endured such opposition from sinners, so that you will not grow weary and lose heart. (Heb. 12:1-3)*

There is no doubt, intentionality is required to accomplish any goal. The author of Hebrews was offering some encouragement to us, trying to help us realize (1) this Christian life may not be easy; (2) we are not alone; and (3) we need to fix our mindset on the goal ahead.

"Fixing our eyes" is an interesting turn of phrase. On the one hand, it means we must firmly set our eyes toward a place, or in this case, a person. Yet, on the other hand, it means we need to correct our vision.

My youngest daughter was around four years of age when we discovered her eyes had issues. One of her eyes would turn in, making it hard to focus and see clearly; it was considered a lazy eye. So, we had to buy some glasses in order to fix her eye and keep it from turning in. She needed to correct her focus so she could see clearly.

Similarly, our view of Jesus and faith can sometimes become a little turned in. Our religious upbringing may have created some legalistic behaviors, and our faith feels stuck. If this happens, our vision goes blurry until we see Him clearly again.

As you fix your eyes on Jesus, you begin to see more clearly. Pride you once held on to, you now see as a roadblock to receiving God's grace. The pain you once felt from your past fades away as you see God's forgiveness transforming you. All these changes are happening because you corrected your focus. Your eyes became fixed on Someone greater than those stumbling blocks!

THROW IT OFF

Distractions abound, don't they? Kids are professional distraction artists! One day I went downstairs to get my daughter so we could leave for school. Her instructions were to go brush her teeth and then come back upstairs so we could leave. Minutes went by, and my patience was evaporating quicker than an ice cube on a midsummer afternoon! I finally went downstairs, only to find she had picked up a stuffed animal and was pretending to brush the animal's invisible teeth!

"*What?! I'm not raising Doc McStuffins*," I thought to myself. I took her animal and told her it was a distraction and that she could play more when we returned from school.

(Okay, that's not entirely true. I got somewhat perturbed and threatened to throw the animal away! But this isn't about my parenting, this is about distractions. Back to the point.)

What are you occupied with? Are there things distracting you, or otherwise hindering you from moving forward? These things may not be sinful or harmful; they may just be distractions. On the surface, they may even seem like good things. Perhaps they are just preferences, or things you enjoy doing. Yet the question remains, are these things hindering you from growing in your faith? Do you need to "throw them off?"

Once, I gave away an Xbox. Oh, no, it's not because I am super generous nor even because I upgraded to a better console. I got rid of it because it was hindering my ability to prioritize my family. My wife and our first daughter needed me more. I truly wanted to be a better dad and husband, and I was being held back by this distraction. I put it off at first, and then justified it for a while, citing how it was my "escape" and "downtime." But honestly, the Xbox had become an excuse to avoid engaging with the people in my life that mattered most. I threw it off.

Distractions are not the only thing the author of Hebrews mentions we need to throw to the side. Look at verse one again, "*let us throw off everything that hinders and the **sin that so easily entangles.*** "(Heb. 12:1)

Sin has a way of trapping us. Sin wants to hold you back like a prisoner. Choices we make that violate God's ways become sin in our life and create a separation between God and us. We must throw it off!

How? You confess your sins to the Lord and receive His forgiveness.[3] By doing so, you are turning away from the wrong focus and moving in a different direction. So, we get rid of the sin and distractions, then we fix our eyes on Jesus.

It all begins with Jesus, and it all ends with Jesus. Jesus initiated faith inside of you. He's the one that's developing that faith inside of you. Jesus is the one that will perfect your faith and make it more mature, again and again. It all begins with Jesus, and it all ends with Jesus. That's why we fix our eyes on Him.

TIRED VS. WEARY

I want you to reflect on your life with me, just for a minute. What are your hobbies, activities, preferences, priorities, and mindsets? Think about the schedule you keep, the endless commitments you have, and the ever-expanding goals you hope to accomplish this year. What things do you wish were different, but feel powerless to change? Think of the many times you attempted to break a particularly difficult habit, and yet you failed again. What about the secret you're holding onto because you don't want anyone to find out about a mistake you once made?

Are you getting weary and tired? Feeling burdened or stressed? Sometimes I wonder if we grow weary because we are striving for things we were never meant to go after. Or maybe we grow weary because there is something we refuse to confess, and it's creating a separation between God and us.

'Tired' is one thing, but 'weary' is different. Tired is a result of hard work. When we are tired, we rest, and the tiredness goes away. Weary is more along the lines of being worn down, wearing thin or losing heart. When we have distractions and sins in our life, we quickly lose heart. When we get consumed with activities that are not life-giving or God-honoring, we become weary. When we try to live in a way that is contrary to our design, we become worn down.

Don't get me wrong. Disappointments are going to come. Things aren't always going to work out the exact way that we desire. There will be times you feel disheartened. Therefore, if we fix our eyes on what surrounds us, we can quickly lose heart. Like air escaping a punctured tire, focusing on things other than Christ shrinks our hope and decreases the size of our passion. But we do not want to become small-hearted or to lose all hope. No matter what the disappointment or the weariness, the key to our strength is still to focus on Jesus, who continuously fills us with His life!

REVERSE OSMOSIS

We purchased a water filtration system for our kitchen. It's pretty sophisticated, having six different stages removing all sorts of unwanted chemicals and minerals. At each step of the process, it filters out the potential contaminants.

I believe Jesus is like that, the perfect filter for our mindset. Put Him at the center of your mindset and crosscheck each thought with the person of Christ. Let your mindset be reflective of His loving nature and His dependable character; of His goodness, His immense power and His unlimited ability. Let us fix and filter everything in our minds through the power of the death, burial, and resurrection of Christ.

Scripture tells us to renew our minds by meditating on God's Word.[4] Biblical meditation is when you talk to yourself, again and again, repeating a scripture, until it soaks into your mindset. We are also told in scripture to take our thoughts captive and submit them to Christ.[5] We need to run every thought we think through the filter of the truth of Jesus. Like a reverse osmosis filtration system for water, God's Word helps remove the toxic mindsets that contaminate our heart.

MARKED COURSE

I've run in a few 5K races over the years, and in every scenario, they have the course marked out and outlined with cones, flags, and people at water stations. Each race has a course marked out for participants to run.

But just because the racecourse has been marked out, doesn't mean every participant is forced to run that path. Runners have a choice to follow the marked track or go off on their own route. However, only the runners who stay on the marked course will qualify for the prize.

I'm sure you see the correlation I'm starting to make. God has marked out a course for your life, but you must choose to stay on the track. Jesus is " ... the way, the truth, and the life"[6] that we are to follow. If we take our eyes off Jesus, the race map for true life, we will get off course. We will also experience a void of something central to satisfaction.

As a person well acquainted with ways of church people (having spent my entire life in the church), I know firsthand how easy it is to get off-course from our race. The Church has been given a course to run by Jesus Himself. We've been charged to hand deliver the Good News[7] that Jesus forgives, saves, redeems, and sets people free! We've been commissioned as ambassadors to be His representatives in the world.[8]

Yet too many church people live with a void of something central to their satisfaction in life. They walk through life without joy, love, passion, or generosity. In place of the fruit of the Spirit, they are full of criticism, gossip, judgmentalism, selfishness, and elitism. This bad fruit is evidence that they've taken their eyes off Jesus and drifted off course.

If we aren't careful, the longer we do the church thing, the blurrier our vision can get. We don't see Jesus nor the world around us as clearly as we used to. Where we used to love worshipping no matter the song, we now only "worship" if we "feel it" or they play our favorite song. We no longer read the Bible with wide-open imaginations and hunger.

The newness wears off of our faith and we quickly dismiss a sermon or Bible story because we are overly familiar with it. It seems like we have done all the Bible studies before. We've accumulated a lot of knowledge. In fact, we can even get to the point where we start thinking Jesus needs to be defended more than experienced! How did we get to this point in our faith? We get to this point when our compass is broken, and we lose sight of Jesus.

But if you put Jesus back at your center, and use His Word as your compass, you can get back on course. With your eyes fixed on His ways, you begin to reflect Him again. You begin living like Jesus, not just defending Him.

That's how the term Christian came to be. The early church was serving, giving and loving others, and the culture around them started to make fun of them, calling them "little Christs." But the early church didn't take that as an insult, they took it as a badge of honor. The word "Christian" literally means "little Christ." I hope we all live in a way that causes people to see Jesus more than they see us! We want His purposes to be on display, not our preferences.

So, what does it look like if we live a life that reflects Jesus? What are the characteristics of a life centered on Him?

SIX CHARACTERISTICS OF A LIFE CENTERED ON JESUS

1. We submit to His leadership.

In Luke 6:46, Jesus stated, "Why do you call me Lord, Lord but yet you don't do anything that I have commanded you?"

When Jesus is the center of our lives, we submit to His leadership. We follow Him. Surrendering to Him means we allow Jesus to take charge, and we set aside our agendas to pursue His. Jesus is the center of our life when we submit to His leadership. Nothing off-limits – no attitude, preference, or hobby. We fully surrender to His direction in our lives.

2. We listen for His voice.

John 10:27 says, "My **sheep** listen to **my voice**; I know them, and they follow me." Hearing God's voice often requires us to turn down some of the other noise in our life so that we can hear Him speak.

It may be some other voices we need to silence – a friend, neighbor, relative, or coach – so we can listen to God clearly. Or it might be we need to turn down the negative self-speak and turn up the whisper of the Lord who says, "I've called you, and I'm equipped you. What you are walking through I can redeem it. Come to Me and let's walk this thing out, together."

When Jesus is the center of our life, His voice will be the most important voice of all.

3. We live with His passion, not our priorities.

Matthew 25:40 says, "Truly I tell you, whatever you did for one of the least of these brothers and sisters of mine, you did for me." God is passionate about taking care of people.

Jesus also told us, "For even the Son of Man did not come to be served, but to serve, and to give his life as a ransom for many." (Mark 10:45)

When Jesus becomes the center of our lives, our passions shift from our selfish desires to His selfless desires to serve. Our priorities begin to bend toward His passions.

4. We steward His authority.

In Matthew 16:19, Jesus says, "I will give you the keys of the kingdom of heaven; whatever you bind on earth will be bound in heaven, and whatever you loose on earth will be loosed in heaven."

Jesus is telling us to pray like God is listening and willing to act. We are sons and daughters of God because of Jesus and our faith in Him.[9] As a result, we have access to all of

God's blessing. His will grants us full access. We steward His authority as we partner with Him to bring about His kingdom on this earth through prayer.

5. We embrace His love.

> *Philippians 3: 8-11 says, " But whatever were gains to me I now consider loss for the sake of Christ. What is more, I consider everything a loss because of the surpassing worth of knowing Christ Jesus my Lord, for whose sake I have lost all things. I consider them garbage, that I may gain Christ and be found in him, not having a righteousness of my own that comes from the law, but that which is through faith in Christ—the righteousness that comes from God on the basis of faith. I want to know Christ—yes, to know the power of his resurrection and participation in his sufferings, becoming like him in his death, and so, somehow, attaining to the resurrection from* **the dead.***"*

This is one of the passages that has deeply impacted me. Paul lists several reasons why he was so respected and accomplished, but then says all his qualifications are worthless compared to knowing Christ. Paul had a mindset with Jesus as the center. Basically, Paul was writing and saying, "Listen, I want to be able to embrace Christ. But if the stuff that I'm holding in my hands – my business, my life, my social status, my education, my 401K – is keeping me from embracing Christ, then it's just garbage." Remember, God is crazy about you! Before you ever heard the name Jesus, He already decided to kill His son for you. All He asks is that we believe in His son. However, even if

Salvation is a free gift that we accept by **believing** right, not by **behaving** right.

#MindsetMattersBook

we believe in Jesus, we cannot embrace God with our arms full of other things.

6. We align our faith to the cross.

Ephesians 2: 8-9 says, "For it is by grace you have been saved, through faith – and this is not from yourselves, it is the gift of God – not by works, so that no one can boast."

When we add stuff to the Gospel, such as, "Believe in Jesus and clean up your act," it's not the Gospel. Salvation is a free gift that we accept by believing right, not by behaving right. There is no such thing as being "good enough" for salvation. He doesn't need your good works.

Isaiah the prophet said it like this, "All of us have become like one who is unclean, and all our righteous acts are like filthy rags. "(Isa. 64:6) Do you want to know the literal translation? It's borderline offensive, but here it is: "Your good works are as valuable as a used menstrual cloth." On our best day, with our best effort, we only achieve the status of a used feminine product, compared to the pure righteousness required to just to be accepted by God.

The good news of salvation is that Jesus steps in to give us His pure righteousness in place of our filthy rags when we put our faith in Him. We respond to His love and receive His life through faith.

It's only Jesus that covers us in His righteousness.[10] All we need is Jesus. He's enough. Christ plus nothing is everything! He's not an add-on to our life, He is the very source of all life. Christ is not an "app" that we download and use when we feel sad or when we hit a tragedy. *Jesus is the operating system through which we live, move, and have our very being!*

Let's keep Jesus at the center and His Word as our compass! Life can get tricky, distracting, and rough at times. But with God's Word fixed in our minds, we can navigate life with joy, perseverance, and clarity, staying on course because we never lose sight of Jesus, our true north. Onward we go!

[3] Make Room

Have you ever had the thought, "*This seems pointless?*" Such a sentiment is not a foreign one to me. The Pythagorean Theorem; making PB&J sandwiches with peanut butter on only one side; making the bed each morning; people who need a warning sign to tell them that getting too close to the ledge of a cliff may result in their death – all of these things seem pretty pointless to me! HA HA! Just kidding ... making the bed is not all that pointless.

All joking aside, purpose in life is a big deal. The book, *The Purpose Driven Life*, written by Rick Warren, sold over 60 million copies worldwide. Those numbers tell me human beings are hungry for purpose! Sadly, most people believe that in order to find their life purpose, they just need to look deeper inside of themselves. I love a good personality test as much as the next person, but ultimately, we will not find our purpose within ourselves.

Everyone has a God-given purpose. I believe God is the Creator. Your parents played a role, but God is the ultimate creative force in our existence. As the Creator, He is best suited to reveal our mission to us. When you come into

Everyone has a God-given **purpose.**

#MindsetMattersBook

agreement with what God is saying about your life, and align your mindset to His purposes, you will begin to realize joy and sense of purpose that is unshakeable.

Did you realize that Jesus had a purpose statement for His life? He set His mind in a specific direction in life and refused to deviate from that purpose. He had a specific mindset that shaped His actions and attitude. This mindset was something specific, and as a result, His life went in that direction. Once Jesus spoke to His disciples about that purpose statement. It went like this:

> *"Jesus called them together and said, "You know that the rulers of the Gentiles lord it over them, and their high officials exercise authority over them. Not so with you. Instead, whoever wants to become great among you must be your servant, and whoever wants to be first must be your slave— just as the Son of Man did not come to be served, but to serve, and to give his life as a ransom for many." (Matt. 20: 25-28)*

What a purpose statement! Did you catch it? Jesus came to serve others first and put His own preferences second. This was the mindset that Jesus had throughout His entire adult life. He calibrated His thoughts to a posture of others first, not self-centeredness.

If anyone ever had the pedigree to be served by others or deserved to live for a self-serving purpose, Jesus did. He is, after all, God's only son. Jesus was there when the first chicken was hatched and the first sunset dazzled. Never once while Jesus was on earth did He sit back and say, "Hey! What's up, people? I'm Lord of Lords and King of Kings. Do as I say!"

No, Jesus came to flip that version of leadership on its head. He redefined greatness as servanthood. He declared that our motivation to be the "first in line" needs to be reversed in His kingdom.

Jesus spent His life making deposits of significance into other people, not withdrawals of selfishness. Jesus epitomized the role of a servant-leader.

And Jesus was a humble servant. Years ago, I heard a pastor say, "The true test of a servant's heart is how they respond when they are treated as a servant." In many religious circles, much emphasis is placed on having a "servant's heart," and rightfully so. Yet, how many leaders of the religious organizations or mega churches do we see acting like servants? We cannot stop at just saying what Jesus said; we must embrace it and calibrate our mindset to do it, to live out His teachings.

PEOPLE OVER PROGRESS

Every person matters. I believe this idea was at the core of Jesus' heart and purpose. I cannot recall one time when Jesus used other people for His own benefit. Time after time, Jesus healed people then instructed them to tell no one. Jesus wasn't trying to build a big following. He was living as a big servant and meeting people's needs, not exploiting them.

Jesus consistently demonstrated the value of human life. He welcomed children that society (and even some of His disciples) tried to push away. He respected women at a time when the societal norm was to dismiss them as second-class. He interacted with the marginalized of humanity – even those whose disease of leprosy required they excuse themselves from normal society. Jesus had a reputation for looking people in their eyes and simply loving them. No matter what they could or couldn't do for Him, His purpose was to serve them.

Perhaps Jesus knew something many of us are just figuring out. Honor is not something we can claim for ourselves; it is something we must give away by placing a value on someone else. In time, if we are worthy, honor will return to us. Until then, you can trust that honoring others never goes out of style and always brings a return on investment. Jesus found a way to deposit honor into someone else's heart in a way that shifted them toward a more enriched purpose.

Jesus valued people over progress. He made room for more people to belong. This is a driving motivation for our church. We are not trying to build a big church; we want to build big people! We want to inspire and equip people, helping their faith grow big on the inside.

RELATIONSHIP + RESPONSIBILITIES

As a follower of Jesus, our mindset needs to be the same as His, so our life moves along His course. This mindset of servanthood and honor, shown to others, is a huge piece to our growth and faith.

There is one story the gospel writers tell about Jesus being in the home of His friends, Mary and Martha. Mary sat with Jesus while Martha worked to serve the guests. While there are many lessons to be gleaned from the story, the need for both relationships and responsibility is evident within this story. Mary modeled the priority of relationship, while Martha embodied the priority of responsibility. We need a little of Mary and a little of Martha in our faith development, too.

If we, like Jesus, are going to make big deposits of God's love into our world we must be diligent with both our relationships and our responsibilities. Relationships are the substance of our life, but it is tending to our responsibilities that moves us forward. Both are fundamental for our growth.

As parents, we can clearly see the need for both relationship and responsibility. If we are going to train and point our children toward the destiny God has designed for them, we must be careful to make sure that we're helping our kids mature relationally and handle responsibility.

If we only cultivate our child's relational abilities and never their ability to handle responsibilities, we end up raising lazy people who are fun to be with but never accomplish anything significant. But if we only emphasize responsibility, without nurturing relationships, we end up raising legalistic people who attempt to control outcomes at the expense of others.

When it comes to our spiritual life of faith, we find the same tension. If we only spend time in relationships but never step up to the responsibilities of discipleship, we produce believers with lots of enthusiasm and emotion, but little practical progress in life.

But if we focus on a discipleship based heavily in responsibilities, leaning more toward "doing" for God rather than "being" like Jesus , we will create believers whose faith goes stale, becomes legalistic and performance-based, and is void of God's grace and power.

At Faith Church, we embrace both relationship and responsibility so we can strengthen our peoples' faith and protect their joy.

We are committed to helping people do three things. We want them to (1) belong to God's family; (2) become a disciple; and (3) build the Kingdom of God together. We want to do these things in the context of relationships, choosing community by participating in a small group. And we want everyone to embrace a responsibility in the church by finding their place on a Serve Team.

Why are we committed to these three things? Because there's nothing that will transform a life of faith like a decision to build Godly relationships, become more like Jesus, and take up responsibility in the kingdom of God. Actively pursue those three things and your strength will soar.

As I write this, I have in mind a couple in our church, who, one day in 2017, found themselves stepping out of their comfort zones to begin serving on our Guest Experience team. They also, perhaps hesitantly, joined a Connect Group. Today, they lead in both those spaces, and their faith, marriage, and outside relationships are thriving. They will tell you that choosing to build relationships while also grabbing a responsibility at church has radically shaped their lives for the better! They are bearing fruit and touching countless lives as they build God's Kingdom.

As we engage in relationships, God moves us beyond our own selfish mindset. Because people matter to God, they matter to us. Soon we truly want other people to feel they belong!

As we choose to sacrifice, accepting responsibility to move things forward in practical ways, we begin to make room for others so that they can belong. We are moved to action.

Make no mistake, helping new people have a sense of belonging is not an easy responsibility to take on. It requires selflessness and transparency. It requires a new mindset. We must be determined to make room. Both individually and organizationally most of us have a natural tendency to stay closed off and keep our world controllable. Yet, this mindset of making room for people to belong is a mindset every follower of Jesus needs to embrace.

Jesus did this all the time. Jesus made room for kids[11] when the disciples had a habit of dismissing them. Jesus took time to go see a little girl who was already dead[12], and then raised her back to life. I'm sure Jesus had a fully packed touring schedule that day, yet He decided to slow down and take care of a grieving family. Other times, He interrupted His "plans" to meet with people who were deemed to be the scum of the earth by other Jews of the day – the tax collectors.[13]

Jesus made room for people to belong. This didn't happen on accident with Jesus, and it won't happen on accident for you and me. We must decide that we are going to make room for people. We must calibrate our thinking in alignment with God's heart. To God, the most precious commodity on earth is people. Humanity is God's most valued creation.

God made room for each of us. And as much as God wanted a relationship with you, He also invites you to be responsible for making room for others to have a relationship with Him, too! He made room in heaven for all of humanity by sending Jesus to pay a price for our lives. God wanted a big family, so He paid the price to make it possible.

DAILY ROOM

So, what does it look like for an individual to courageously live out a mindset of making room for other people to belong to Christ? How can a stay-at-home mom make room for other people? How can a student shoulder responsibility to make more room for others?
Five ways to make room for other people to belong

1. Make room for people in your prayers.

In your own mind, identify the last three prayer requests you made to the Lord. Were they about you or were they on behalf of somebody else? What if we decided to start making room for people just in our prayers?

God does not have a problem with you asking for things you need. In fact, He wants you to bring your requests to Him. He longs to demonstrate His goodness toward you. But you can imagine His delight when you make room for others in your prayers, too.
When we first moved into our current neighborhood, we initially met a couple of our neighbors, but after we got settled in, I realized that there were several that we hadn't yet met. Even though I hadn't met them yet, I began praying for those neighbors. I didn't know their stories, I didn't know where they worked, and I didn't know what was going on in their spiritual lives. I just began to pray for them, because I knew they mattered to God. I began making room for them in my prayers.

Jesus often withdrew to pray. I don't think it'd be a stretch to assume He often prayed for other people in addition to

His own concerns. He wasn't self-centered, so His prayers weren't self-centered either. Let's be like Jesus. Let's make room for other people in our prayers.

2. Make room for people in your schedules.

I get it. None of us like to be inconvenienced by stuff that we weren't planning on doing. Right? I don't even want to get interrupted from my couch time long enough to go get somebody else a glass of milk! To be even more transparent, sometimes I'm only willing to be inconvenienced if someone else is going to notice my "sacrifice."

One thing I've noticed about the community where I live is that people have everything timed down to the minute. They know it only takes six minutes to get from one elementary school to the next elementary school, and they count on every minute when they take their kids to school each day. But all it takes is one slow moving train (which happens with amazing regularity), one person from out-of-town who gets in your way, or one minivan that cannot get their automatic door to work right in the car line to throw your whole schedule off! Why?

Tiny delays can throw off our entire schedule for the morning because we don't factor in time for something called "margin" in our life. Instead, we live life from edge to edge, timewise. When we don't schedule any margin – a small cushion of time in case something doesn't go according to plan – we also end up squeezing the Holy Spirit right out of our lives. With no margin, we have no space for divine interruptions. We miss opportunities to show God's love or serve others consistently. This is because our schedule is over-focused on our priorities, and under-focused on God's priority: people.

As a pastor, there are lots of things I like to accomplish. I'm pretty task oriented. I like progress and completion. I love surrounding myself with people who are inclined to take action. But there are days in my schedule that I have intentionally blocked out just to meet with people. I sometimes don't even know who they will be ahead of time, but I've made room for them. It may be a week or two before I can meet with someone, but I will make room for them. Time, like money, must be budgeted. What if we all started budgeting our time with enough margin to allow for unexpected opportunities to serve other people? Let's make room for people in our schedules – both planned and spontaneous.

3. Make room for people in your preferences.

I remember a time when our oldest daughter was eight years old. My wife and I were preparing to leave for the evening, and she came in with a serious question, "Dad, who's going to be here with us?"

So, being the fun-loving dad that I am, I decided to play a game with her. "Baby, we're going to leave you guys all by yourselves. You're here, so you can watch your brother and your sister. I'm sure you'll be alright."

God always **meets us** at our point of **surrender.**

#MindsetMattersBook

Being a typical older child, she began processing this aloud, immediately. "What?! No, you've got to have somebody to watch us," she objected. I could see her practical brain starting to think, *"My brother doesn't listen to me, I know this isn't going to work out so well. He's gonna do the wrong thing and then I'm going to get in trouble. I'm scared."*

Of course, I didn't keep going. I quickly came clean and told her that we had someone coming over to be with them. She was relieved, but what came next still makes me laugh to this day! Within moments of being reassured she wouldn't be left alone and in charge; she spoke up again.

"Hey dad, if you left, and mom left, and nobody else was here to watch us, and I WAS watching us all – does that make me the ruler? Because I'd like to be a ruler. Like, I would be in charge, and my brother and sister would have to do what I tell them, right? I'd get to be the ruler, right?"

I'm sure you can relate. We all like control. We like what we like. We have opinions and rarely do we hesitate to make them known. There seems to be a sense of true delight in being in charge and not answering to others.

But if we are not careful, our desire to be in charge can get in the way of making room for other people to belong. We all have preferences for how to run things, but to tell the truth we must lay aside some of our preferences in order to serve others, especially if we call Jesus "Lord." If He is Lord, then we are not. He gets to set the preferences and priorities as we deal with other people, not us.

Jesus gets to be the one that calls the shots in our lives, including having a say in how we treat our spouse. What preferences do you have that crowd out others and focus only on you? Or how do you plan to spend your weekend? Is there room for your family's needs, or just your hobbies? What is your preferred sense of humor at work? Do your jokes keep people from seeing Jesus clearly and accurately when they hear you?

Allowing Jesus to be Lord in our lives starts with our preferences. Do you have any preferences that don't align with Jesus? Are any of those preferences hindering you from making room for others?

Jesus wants to have a say about the kind of thoughts we think. He wants to have a say in how we manage our time and what we prioritize. When we prayed, "Jesus, please be my Lord," He honestly believed that we meant it.

Jesus invites us to participate in His mission of making room for people in God's family. Jesus came to model servanthood as the primary method of making room for others. The call to follow Jesus is a call to be a servant, like Him. I've heard it said, "The true test of a "servant's heart" is how a person responds when they are actually treated like a servant." How do you respond when God lovingly asks you to lay aside your preferences and serve in the way needed most now?

In a church, you usually don't have to look very far to notice people's preferences. Most of the time we don't call it preference, that would be too honest. So, in church we dress up our preferences for a lot of things, and just call it our "personality."

For example, look at worship style.

Some like worship to be more liturgical, while other people like it to be more contemporary. The only real issue with either style is a preference. Worship is an expression of adoration and love. Did you know God has a love language, just like people have love languages? He has defined what is worship to Him; He tells us how to worship. He tells us He prefers people to worship in Spirit and Truth.[14]

The Bible also tells us to dance, sing, shout, clap, use stringed instruments, percussion instruments, wind instruments, kneel or bow, and lift up our hands, along with other directives! God, as the subject of worship, gets to define how He likes to be worshipped! Even if these different worship styles make us personally uncomfortable, our preferences must be surrendered to His preferences.

God always meets us at our point of surrender. You will be more satisfied with your worship, faith and relationship with God when you choose to surrender your preferences to His. As followers of Jesus, we must set our preferences aside and say, "God, we want to make room for You and for your people, no matter what it takes."

4. Make room for people in your circle of friends.

When was the last time you invited somebody new to go to the park with you and your family? When was the last time you invited somebody to church? When was the last time you invited someone to grab a coffee? What if you decided to make room in your circle of friends to include somebody else? They may not think the same, act the same, dress the same, look the same or have the same background as you. But can you imagine all the good that could happen if we all extended our circle and invited at least one person or family in and gave them a place to belong?

5. Make room for people in our conversations.

Too often we make assumptions about people while in conversation. We take their words as intentionally rude and assume they are just jerks. But what if we gave them a little grace and allowed them to be human? Sometimes people come off as rude when they are just stressed out or hurt. You'd want someone to give you the benefit of the doubt in such a situation, so make room for them, too.

We need to make up our minds that we will make room for people to belong at church. That means there may be people who show up in our lives who are not like us. There will be people whose life is a little messier than ours. Maybe they didn't grow up in church at all. Or maybe they did, but they don't know what it means to lift their hands in worship. Some don't even know where the book of Genesis is located in their Bible. But what if we decided we're going to make room for people who are unlike us to belong in our church? Once we make that decision, we begin to see them for who they are, explain things to them along the way, and generally care about them.

Jesus said, "The harvest is plentiful, but the workers are few. Ask the Lord of the harvest, therefore, to send out workers into his harvest field." (Matt. 9:37-38) He was talking about a harvest of people, people who need hope and salvation.

There's more work to be done and more workers needed in God's kingdom. Make no mistake, making room for people to belong is inconvenient. Making room for people to belong requires some sacrifice. But it is also a commitment the Lord calls us to make – a conscientious choice to serve others first. And it's all worth it someday when you hear somebody say, "Hey, you changed my life! Thank you so much for inviting me! I found a new home. Thank you so much for praying for me; everything has changed."

We all have a part to play in the body of Christ. We can all make room for someone to belong. We can all serve like Jesus served, following in His footsteps. Your mindset matters. A mindset that sets aside our preferences so others can belong is a mindset that will fill your life with purpose and joy.

[4] Committed Contributor

Let me tell you a parable.

"This tale is about four young lads by the name of Somebody, Everybody, Anybody, and Nobody. Together they were the best of friends. But I must confess when it came to getting a job done, they weren't very good. You see, whenever they were given a job, Everybody was sure that Somebody would do it and Anybody could have done it. But in the end, Nobody always ended up with the task. When Nobody did it, Somebody was angry because it was Everybody's job, but Everybody thought that Somebody would do it instead. Now Nobody realized that Nobody would do it, so consequently Everybody blamed Somebody when Nobody did what Anybody could have done in the first place.
Now as you may have guessed these four were fun, active, busy people. But what little they accomplished was a shame, and everyone knew it. You see Everybody had a good idea, but Everybody thought Somebody would follow it through. However, Somebody thought that Anybody would work on it and Anybody thought Everybody should do it. So, Nobody

ended up working on it, once again.

Now I have one last tale to tell. You see all the boys work at a firm. And at this firm worked Someone Else. Now the four were greatly saddened to learn of the death of one of the most valuable members, Someone Else. Someone's passing created a vacancy that will be difficult to fill. He had been around for years and for every one of those years Someone Else did far more than a normal person's share of work. Whenever Anybody mentioned leadership, Somebody always looked to this wonderful person, Someone Else, for inspiration and results. When there was a job to be done that needed a place of leadership to be filled, one name was always given: Someone Else. Everyone knew Someone Else was the largest giver of time and money. Whenever there was a financial need, Everybody, Anybody, and Somebody always assumed that Someone Else would make up the difference. Now Someone Else is gone and the boys all wonder what they will do. No longer can they utter the words, "Let Someone Else do it." If it is going to be done, one of them will now have to do it. And I guess that most of the time, it will being Nobody that gets it done."[15]

Some of you moms are reading this thinking, "You just described my household perfectly!" It reminds me of a saying that's going around my house right now, "But I didn't make that mess."

I ask my children to take something downstairs to the playroom, "But I didn't bring that up here," they reply. Somehow, my words, "Will you please take this downstairs?" in their mind became, "Hey if you played with this for at least five minutes, or if you brought it up here, or if you were the last one to touch it, take it downstairs."

We can see the toxic "it's not my mess" mindset all around us – at work, at home, and even at church! No one wants to take responsibility, but everyone sure would like someone else to!

From post-game snack duties on our kid's soccer team to the upkeep of the common areas in our neighborhood, we are glad those items are cared for, we just don't want to contribute to their upkeep.

And that mindset can easily creep in for anyone and cause a major rift with those around them, quietly embedding consumerist thinking and lazy, selfish behavior into our lives. Can you imagine what your house would look like if the attitude of, "that's not my mess," became everyone's mindset?

There's a phrase I heard many years ago from Andy Stanley that goes something like "If I don't_____, we won't _____." It's a fill-in-the-blank mantra for the organization he leads, designed to help people understand the long-term results of not taking responsibility. For example, "If I don't pick up the trash on the ground, we won't have a clean facility," is one application; here is another, "If I don't organize the stockroom, we won't be able to find what we need."

Andy's fill-in-the-blank mantra helped everyone take ownership of the company. The idea was to shift from "me" thinking to "we" thinking, moving the team from passive to proactive – and it worked.

VICTIM MINDSET

There is a mindset many of us have embedded in our lives. It's formed in the earliest years of our upbringing, reinforced by the surrounding culture, and amplified by personal sinfulness. Many live with this mentality driving their life. What is this negative mindset? It's the idea that we are the victim in our story.

This way of thinking creates grooves that grab hold of the tires of our lives and keep us from gaining the traction needed to move ahead to success. As a victim, we feel stuck and trapped. We begin to react selfishly as a protective mechanism, just hoping we will somehow survive.

This victim mindset comes with a tainted perspective, a filter that rejects personal responsibility and casts blame on others in our life.

The voice of the victim mindset sounds like:
- "If my parents weren't so strict, I'd have more fun in life."
- "If my kids weren't so crazy, I wouldn't be late all the time."
- "If my boss weren't so controlling, I could really be a help to this firm."

It's not difficult to spot the victim mindset in others, but it is nearly impossible to see it within yourself. But, if we're honest, we all have some tendency to think this way.

I am convinced God gave us the local Church to help reset this pre-programmed victim mindset within us. There is something good that occurs in us when we intentionally sacrifice and spend time serving others in our community. These actions sharpen away our self-centered way of thinking. The key to maturity is to shift our focus off ourselves, and shift our worship onto God.

TRUE WORSHIP

You cannot do the same thing over and over again, expecting different results. If you want a different outcome, you must change what you input. If you want the results in your life to change, you have change what thoughts you allow into your mind.

One of my life verses is found in the book of Romans:
"Therefore, I urge you, brothers and sisters, in view of God's mercy, to offer your bodies as a living sacrifice, holy and pleasing to God—this is your true and proper worship. Do not conform to the pattern of this world but be transformed by the renewing of your mind. Then you will be able to test and approve what God's will is—his good, pleasing and perfect will." (Rom. 12:1-2)

If you want a different **outcome**, you must change what you **input**.

#MindsetMattersBook

Paul was writing to a Roman audience, a group of people who lived in an influential city. The city of Rome was powerful, wealthy, and an epicenter of culture. If Rome said it or created it, it was impressive. They were the model that everyone followed. In fact, the Roman Empire set the standard that shaped the ideology of their time, clear across Europe.

Due to this influence, Paul writes, warning Roman believers (and us) about going along with the pre-programmed culture. He uses phrases like "I urge you" to emphasize the critical nature of his statements. Why? Because if we miss this starting point, we will be off target in the end.

Your life is your worship. All of it. The truest form of worship is not a song or a style, but it is you, surrendered in everything to God's priority. Your mindset affects your worship. Think about it. Romans says our life is worship. Again, "...I urge you, brothers and sisters ... to offer your bodies as a living sacrifice, holy and pleasing to God—this is your true and proper worship." (Rom. 12:1)

So, if our life is self-centered, our worship is small and shallow. But if our mindset shifts to God, it is large and deep, producing a Christ-honoring life.

CONSUMER CULTURE

It's easy to be influenced by the culture around us. The environment of society has a strong opinion on how to build your life. It has ideas on how to handle money, deal with relationship conflict or how to interact with society, as a whole.

We live in a culture that thinks if we don't get something for ourselves now, we won't ever get it. The drive is to go for it now and ask questions later. We live in an environment that convinces us our personal preferences are the most important things to consider, and our pleasure is the ultimate gauge for satisfaction in life.

Yet while so many people seem to believe that pleasure is the ultimate gauge for satisfaction in life, the majority are not happy at all. Instead, they are stuck in their selfishness, living without passion, purpose, or a sense of honest fulfillment. Why? I think it is because their chief aim is to be self-fulfilled and not need anyone else to get all you can get. This is distinctly different from the way of Jesus.

To put it another way, we were designed to be committed contributors worshiping God, not casual consumers, living solely for our own self-pleasure. People's tendency, however, is to conform their lives to what the world does, filtering life's decisions through a decision-making grid designed to limit the demands of personal responsibility, inconvenience, and personal commitment on our lives.

The me-first consumer mindset must be laid down if it is to be renewed to God's purpose. This is essential because the pattern of thinking you possess determines the purpose you live out. Your mindset matters. Whether consumer driven or contributor-motivated, your pattern of living reveals your mindset.

We all have mindsets that have been constructed by our culture that must be reset by the cross of Christ. These mindsets must be reset, wiped clean and started over, based on what the cross of Christ tells us and the message of the Gospel. The life, sacrifice, and righteousness of Jesus can filter out patterns of thinking that are toxic to our future. It is necessary to renew our minds and not allow negative thinking to remain in our life.

In the Western world, we live in a society and culture that is very much consumer-driven and consumer-oriented. Let's take relationships for example. We keep the relationship that meets our needs and distance ourselves from the ones that don't. Relationships have become a commodity we can swipe right through if they don't meet our internal metrics. I realize that relationships are complex and certainly don't want to brush past the negative realities many people have experienced. But at the core of many negative issues in relationships, the base problem comes down to a matter of selfishness. This is made worse by the cultural mindset that says, "We're here to consume and if the goods I'm getting from you aren't what I want, then I'll start shopping."

This consumerist attitude has crept into the Church. We even have a term for it, "Church shopping." Church shopping looks like this: we quit going to Church X because we don't feel like we were "getting fed." Perhaps we don't like a music style, or the church doesn't have the programs we are accustomed to, or something else we feel we deserve. We put our comfortableness with the church above the mission.

True, finding a church home is no easy task. It's a bit intimidating to try and find a place to call 'home.' There are so many questions and fears for people seeking a new church. Inside of every visitor's mind are dozens of questions, like "Will I get weird looks? What if they make me stand up and talk? Do I have to sign a contract? Are my kids gonna find a friend? Am I dressed right?"

At our church, we work hard to give people the blessing of anonymity, while trying to make it easy for them to become better known to others when they are ready. We want to create a life-giving experience for every person, no matter their previous background.
As a pastor, I want to see people flourish as they encounter God's best. I have witnessed that when a person gets connected to the right church environment, they begin to grow and flourish. Finding the right church home is more about being where God wants you to be planted than where your preferences are appeased. You truly begin to flourish when you recognize you have a relationship to contribute to this church body and a responsibility to carry there, as well.

But we cannot turn Church into a "consumable good" for ourselves, rather than an opportunity to serve God, to contribute. We must take strides to be committed contributors, not casual consumers.

CONTRAST

May I offer a few contrasting thoughts? I think it will help underscore this consumer versus contributor idea.

First, a consumer mindset expects entertainment, while a contributor mindset excels in engagement.

This mentality shows up when I come home after a day of work and I am ready to sit in front of the TV for a little while. But what is more important is that when I come home, I engage with my kids and family. What I really want to do is sit back and be entertained, but what's more important is that I am a God-honoring father and a husband that loves and serves his wife.

If you take a few minutes to review your last three days, you will likely identify moments where you chose entertainment over engagement. Engagement requires sacrifice upfront, but the payoff is on the backside.

By contrast, entertainment offers its benefits upfront, but regrets, a time crunch, and/or stress make up the payoff negative on the back-half. Whether a consumer or a contributor, both have their payoffs, and both have their price.

Second, a consumer mindset causes us to focus on comparisons, but a contributing mindset focuses on the cause.

> A **consumer** mindset expects entertainment, while a **contributor** mindset excels in engagement.

#MindsetMattersBook

The driving force of consumerism is never being satisfied, leading us to jealousy. I believe criticism is the language of comparison. If you look around at your life, and begin comparing it to someone else's life, you'll soon start criticizing them. This leads you to arrogance or the opposite, self-criticism. Arrogance and self-criticism are both displays of personal insecurity.

On the flip side, when you choose to be a contributor instead of a consumer, your heart tracks with the mission to which you are contributing. You get focused on doing your part and don't have time to compare your life to others.

Finally, just because we're not consumers, doesn't mean that we can become careless or sloppy in our approach.

Instead, I think contributing should lead us to cultivate diligence. Webster's defines diligence as "careful and persistent work or effort."[16] When we are caring and aware of the produce of our lives, we honor God. The Bible tells us to "taste and see that the Lord is good." How do people taste God's goodness? They taste God's goodness when His people, who are diligent to let the fruit of His Spirit grow in their lives, reach out to serve them with excellence and care. Growing produce requires diligence.

Our very lives should shout the excellence and goodness of God, not our own perfection or showiness, but instead, fruitfulness. We need to put our best foot forward as often as possible.

When we live as contributors, it leads us to care more, not to settle for less. God wants His best for you, and you should give God your best, too. If you're a craftsman, care about the process from beginning to end. If you're a salesman, value people and treat everyone with world-class honor. If you're a teacher, prepare your lessons as if you're training a future president. We need to be diligent in every arena of our lives, including in how we serve God.

"Yeah. But Pastor, that's so external! Doesn't the Bible say that God looks at the heart? Does God really care if everything we do is excellent, styled, and good-looking?"

He absolutely does.

But if you don't care what your service to God looks like, and instead your heart says, "I'm here to consume (and barely contribute) so I can feel good about me," then I would say it's time to check out that heart! While God looks at the heart, mankind looks at the fruit on display; and will judge the authenticity of your faith by your actions. People need a savior, so draw them to God by your good works![17]

As a church, we are trying to reach people, people who naturally gravitate toward being consumers. And so, our actions really matter. We want to do everything to the best of our ability; to contribute to the work of God according to our gifting and capacity so all can be done with excellence. God is glorified and people are impacted as we strive toward excellence with a sincere heart!

YOUR PART MATTERS

It was Saint Irenaeus who said, "The glory of God is man fully alive."[18] I hope you become fully alive to the mission God has for you. I can tell you from my own life, you will feel most alive when you live as a committed contributor, not a casual consumer.

You have something to offer. Don't compare or criticize the gifts God has given you, find creative ways to leverage them. Make a habit of serving with your full capacity - your energy, emotion, intelligence, and strength. Serve with a heart of diligence, using your gift for God's glory.

Look at Romans 12:3-5:
> *"For by the grace was given me I say to every one of you: Do not think of yourself more highly than you ought, but rather think of yourself with sober judgment, in accordance with the faith God has distributed to each of you. For just as each of us has one body with many members, and these members do not all have the same function, so in Christ, we, though many, form one body, and each member belongs to all the others."*

Your part is significant. You are not too young nor old, too busy nor too important. If Paul were talking to us today, he might say something like, "Come on, y'all. Be real about this; you're not too busy to make a difference. You are not too important to contribute. You have not been disqualified from participating by something that happened in your past. You ALL have a role, some more visible than others, so

Don't **compare** or **criticize** the gifts God has given you, find **creative ways** to leverage them.

#MindsetMattersBook

stop comparing and start contributing toward the mission of Jesus!"

Let's contribute our best to God, and then consume from whatever is left over. Let's not consume first and contribute our leftovers to God. It's time to shift our mindsets to say, "We are committed contributors, not casual consumers."

Years ago, our oldest daughter was in second grade. Wintertime was coming in North Carolina, where we were living at the time. It doesn't typically get very cold in North Carolina, but it was getting pretty cold that year. Our daughter came home telling us that there were kids in her class who didn't have proper attire for the weather. As she was explaining the scenario to us, she suddenly looked at us and said, "We've got extras. Can I bring our extra hats and scarves and gloves?" Can I also bring a few coats and give them away?"

We thought it was a great idea, so she took our extras to her classroom and gave them to her teacher, who began to distribute them as needed. I was super proud of her for making the choice to contribute, not just consume.
But that's not the end of the story. Fast forward a couple of months and my daughter was out on the playground. She saw her teacher and asked, "Where do you go to church?"

"Well," her teacher said, "I don't really go to church right now."

"You should come to my church," my daughter said. "It's great." Then she went off and played.

The next day, my daughter brought her teacher a church pen and an invite card.

Eventually, her teacher came to our church, surrendered her life to Jesus, was baptized along with her daughter, and even began serving!

What an example that no one is too young or otherwise unqualified to serve Jesus! Never despise your contribution! Never settle for just consuming!

What if we all decided not to be casual consumers anymore? What if we all decided to live as committed contributors and it became the number one priority of our life? Can you imagine what God could do?

What contribution have you been holding back? Maybe it's time to jump in and start giving, and just see what God does with it! Remember, your part is essential. In the Body of Christ there are no insignificant parts.

[5] Focus

I really don't enjoy going to new restaurants. I mean, don't get me wrong, I like good food and trying new things, but new eating spots stress me out a little bit. It's all the unknowns, questions, and crazy thoughts that trigger my anxiety.

My thoughts go something like this: *Will the place be clean? I hope it's not crowded. How much will this cost? What if I order something I don't like? What will I order? I hope we don't get a rude waiter!*

I remember one experience that illustrates why I have a hesitation about trying new restaurants. Some years back, when we lived in Charlotte, North Carolina, My wife and I were invited to join some friends for dinner at an Italian spot in downtown Charlotte. We didn't do that very often, but since we were going with friends that had been to this restaurant before, we were excited to go.

Now, Charlotte is a big city, and downtown is filled with one-way streets, an absurd number of traffic lights, high parking prices, a low number of convenient parking spots, and poorly designed signage. Needless to say, we got lost.

Okay, I got lost.
Finally, we found the restaurant, but we couldn't find a place to park. We ended up parking several blocks away. We hadn't even stepped foot in the place, and I was already frustrated.

But my wife looked gorgeous, we had no kids with us, and the weather was perfect. So, I resolved to keep a peaceful mindset and determined to have a good time.

When we walked into the restaurant, it smelled great. I saw plenty of room. I loved the trendy and clean vibe. Things were looking up.

Then the hostess greeted us and asked if we'd ever been there before (Was it that obvious?). With auctioneer-like speed, she oriented us to the ordering experience upon which we were about to embark. To order, we would need to use a swipe-card, which she supplied. The restaurant had various food and beverage stations, and we could swipe the card at any food or beverage station, order what we wanted, and wait as they cooked it fresh right there before our eyes. We could sit wherever we wanted. At the end of this dining experience, we were to bring the swipe-card to the hostess in order to pay for our meals.

There was no waiter. No menu. And no clear prices on any of the food. The whole experience seemed like a funky combo of a high school cafeteria mixed with an overstimulated arcade. It took me almost twenty minutes to order. Did I want a pizza or pasta? What's this gonna cost me? Even when I finally decided on pasta, I had to pick my type of noodle from a list that included more noodles than I even knew existed.

This was all followed by picking a homemade sauce from a long list, then choosing from a list of meats, and so on. I let so many people skip ahead of me in line it was sad! Don't get me wrong, the food was amazing. But I was crippled by the multiplicity of options, and my brain was overloaded trying not to pick something for dinner that I'd regret later.

In America, we live in such a prosperous land that even our prosperity can become problematic. Just try walking down the grocery store aisle looking for a particular type of salad dressing. Not only do you have the main name brand version of that item, but you have the generic brand of the same.

Likely, there are a copious number of other name brands, as well. Now add in flavors, organic varieties, diet/light versions, and gluten-free options and you are on overload just trying to find a salad dressing. Is it any wonder that most of us have a problem with focus?

ROCK, PAPER, SCISSORS.

As a teen, any time my friends and I were stalled in making a choice, we played "Rock, Paper, Scissors."

What did we do if we couldn't decide which video game to play? Rock, Paper, Scissors. How did we decide where to go for an off-campus lunch? Rock, Paper, Scissors. This simple little game helped us decide so many things.

When it comes to the weightier decisions in our lives, so many options to choose from is confusing. We are afraid to fail, but we certainly don't want to miss out. We can find ourselves in a place where we can't even make a decision. What are we to do – play Rock, Paper, Scissors for every decision? That game may work well for selecting who goes first in kickball, but it's not a great way to select a spouse. Nor is it a great way to decide which college to attend, what job to take, which church to join, or what house to buy. An estimated 20 to 50 percent of students enter college as "undecided" majors and an estimated 75 percent of students change their major even after they've decided, at least once before graduation.[19] With so many choices today, young people can find themselves too afraid to even start!

VALUE-BASED DECISIONS.

What is the answer for a culture overrun with options, activities, and commitments? How do we move beyond the paralysis and the fear we have when making decisions? I believe the grid for making good decisions is found when we anchor to a purpose greater than self-satisfaction. When our values are Godly, they can help us filter every priority to a more eternal purpose. We can confidently narrow our focus and avoid the side-show of distractions that can easily trap us unknowingly in a life without true purpose.

"When our **values** are Godly, they can help us filter every priority to an **eternal purpose.**

#MindsetMattersBook

The church isn't immune to this overload of options. With so many programs, committees, opportunities, slogans, Bible studies to attend, and fellowship outings to engage in, many people sit idle, wondering where to begin. People need a clear path, more than they need more options. Perhaps that's why Jesus' first invitation was simply "Follow Me."

At Faith Church, we want to keep things simple and streamlined. We want to make a clear pathway to help people follow Jesus, helping them take their first steps. Our approach as a church is to focus on a few things and do them well.

We've narrowed our mission focus and shaped the way we approach ministry around our values (we call them mindsets). Because we have settled our mindset and aligned it to our mission, we can put all our energy into accomplishing that mission.

Values help clarify what matters and what doesn't matter. Values are at the core of who you are called to be. I once heard a church leader say, "As you try and determine if something should be a core value of your church or not, ask yourself, "Is this a value I am willing to let people leave our church over?"

Values-based decision making helps you determine what your priorities will be for your life, your family, or your organization. For instance, having a value of honoring others and helping others see value in themselves helps you pre-decide to treat even the local cashier with kindness, no matter what you think about their job performance. Values guide you to live with clarity and focus despite the circumstances.

I love the Disney Pixar movie, The Incredibles. There is a scene where the mom tries to reason with her son by saying, "Everyone is special." The son quickly mumbles, "That's just a way of saying no one is special." In a way, the son is right. The tricky thing about priorities is you must decide what isn't most important. Having priorities means you eventually must decide not only what is most special, important, valuable, and effective – and what is not.

As a Christ-follower, I believe the best priorities in life are shaped by God's perspective. In Isaiah chapter 55 we read about God's vantage point.

> *"Why spend money on what is not bread, and your labor on what does not satisfy? Listen, listen to me, and eat what is good, and you will delight in the richest of fare. Give ear and come to me; listen, that you may live. I will make an everlasting covenant with you, my faithful love promised to David. ... Seek the Lord while he may be found; call on him while he is near. Let the wicked forsake their ways and the unrighteous their thoughts. Let them turn to the Lord, and he will have mercy on them, and to our God, for he will freely pardon. "For my thoughts are not your thoughts, neither are your ways my ways," declares the Lord. "As the heavens are higher than the earth, so are my ways higher than your*

> *ways and my thoughts than your thoughts. As the rain and the snow come down from heaven, and do not return to it without watering the earth and making it bud and flourish, so that it yields seed for the sower and bread for the eater, so is my word that goes out from my mouth: It will not return to me empty, but will accomplish what I desire and achieve the purpose for which I sent it. You will go out in joy and be led forth in peace; the mountains and hills will burst into song before you, and all the trees of the field will clap their hands." (Is. 55:2-12)*

Notice that when we align our priorities to God's, we are promised delight, satisfaction, and provision for today, as well as seed that provides for tomorrow. There is a peace that accompanies God's pattern of living. God's priorities, values, and thoughts are higher than ours.

A mindset shift needs to occur in our thinking if we are to align ourselves with God's priorities.

If we are being honest, we must acknowledge that our life isn't always full of peace, satisfaction, and delight. Often, we feel like we are missing something. According to Isaiah 55, God is not the problem. If God is not the problem, then something needs to change with us. Again, the problem is mindset. We will walk in God's abundance and blessing and receive the promises of God for our lives when we align our mindset to what matters most to God.

But how do we do that? What do we need to focus on in order to better align ourselves with God's mindset and see a shift from dissatisfaction to fulfillment in life?

Allow me to offer two thoughts on this subject.

First, we must be clear about our purpose.

Why am I here? What is my purpose? These are two questions that most people struggle to answer. Because so many people live with a lack of understanding of what their purpose is, they can't live focused lives. They are scattered at best.

If we have no purpose, whatever mood we wake up with determines our priorities that day. We switch schools, majors, jobs, and spouses all because we still don't feel a sense of purpose.

Why?

Because we confuse personal pursuit with true purpose. We are not driven by Godly priorities.

At the very beginning of those verses we read, ""Why spend money on what is not bread, and your labor on what does not satisfy?" [20]

God was trying to get the Israelites to realize their spending decisions were focused on things that would only temporarily satisfy. They spent their money on a selfish substitute that didn't last. Their misplaced priorities were leaving them empty on the inside.

May I suggest that if you are feeling empty, or lost without a purpose, that perhaps you too have been grabbing for "substitute bread?" There is a purpose higher than the one you've been pursuing. When we chase our preferences instead of our purpose, we end up living a life with far less meaning than God desires.

Others of us feel we are living with purpose because we are so busy. But just because we are busy and have full schedules, doesn't mean we are living with purpose. If we have this mindset, when we find ourselves unfulfilled, we add another activity or change activities, we may just find ourselves worn out with unfulfilling lives someday. Activity isn't the same thing as purpose, and it doesn't automatically produce fruitful, fulfilling lives.

I even see this all the time in the church, among Christ-followers. They assume because they attend lots of activities at church, they are growing. But it's possible to attend church your whole life and not actually grow in the Lord. Unless we are proactive in surrendering our busy pursuits to be aligned with God's purposes, we will be substituting church activity for fulfillment. We may look good on the outside, but we will not flourish on the inside.

Similarly, many confuse "opportunities" with direction and purpose. An opportunity presents itself to us, perhaps a job offer or a new relationship. Immediately we think,

"Oh, here's an open door. This must be God's purpose for my life." But not every open door is from God. And not every relationship opportunity that comes your way is an opportunity that you should step into.

Just because you CAN do something doesn't mean you should! Just because your kids can play that sport doesn't mean that they should play that sport. Just because you can eat a "heart attack on a bun" doesn't mean you should eat it! Just because you could add a new product to your business line, doesn't mean you need to add it right now.

The devil would rather us be busy and unsatisfied than focused and living out our purpose. Most of us have spent so long catering to our personal pursuits, that we have a hard time distinguishing God's purposes from our own. Because of this, we sometimes live our life absent of the conviction necessary to know the right direction we should go.

Second, we must develop God-honoring priorities.

Have you ever had a hard time saying "no?" Many people find that difficult. No one wants to disappoint a friend, and no one likes the idea that they might miss out on something fun. Deep within each of us is a desire to belong. And so, we continue to say "Yes" again and again, often when we really should say "no."

However, by always saying "yes" we inadvertently become slaves to the urgent, rather than tending to the important.

Anything we are **unwilling** to surrender to God is an **idol** in our lives.

#MindsetMattersBook

We lose focus because we're busy pleasing people rather than living by Godly priorities. We end up spreading ourselves too thin and have no margin in our lives for things that help us align with our priorities and accomplish our purpose.

When I am living without focus and my priorities are misaligned, I live with a "God-complex." This complex is a mindset that strives to control others yet is motivated by the need to be needed by them. When someone needs to control others but still needs others' approval at the same time, it is easy to get confused. Pleasing people all the time, however, is a sure way to get off track. Again, remember, it is OK to say no. God wants us to steward our lives and align our priorities in a way that honors Him.

We say we love God first but do our time, talent, and treasure reflect that value? You might intend to live with a God-first priority, but our intentions are not enough. It's the actual investment of our time that reveals our priorities.

Let's say your priority is to have a passionate love life with your spouse and be sincere in your intentions. Yet if you never give them compliments, always nag, and never calendar a date, your actions reveal your real priority. You can say it's your intention, but until your behavior comes into alignment, your priority is not the passion-filled marriage you claim to desire.

Anything we are unwilling to surrender to God is an idol in our lives. This isn't a popular statement, but it is true, nonetheless. What if God asks you to not put your kids in any more extra-curricular sports for one year? Would you do it? Or what if you need to surrender social media for a year so you can focus on school? Can you survive? Let's say God wants you to prioritize your marriage, and you need to stop fishing (or whatever hobby) for a summer, in order to make time with your spouse.

Are you willing?

All I'm trying to communicate is that many times we want it both ways, and to have it all, all at once! We want to fill our time with hobbies yet see our homes blessed and flourishing at the same time. We want to say "Yes" to every opportunity, yet never be worn out. However, the truth is that we can't do it all, all at once. At some point, we must intentionally focus our lives around the priorities that produce God's best, or we will be exhausted. To accomplish this in the long run we may need to remove some "idols" from our lives that we've allowed to take root in our hearts.

Here is the bottom line: the fruit of God's promises are the result of living with God's priorities. Living with the right purpose brings real satisfaction. Go back and reread Isaiah 55. *"The blessing and provision promised in that Scripture are conditional on living with God's purposes and priorities as number one in our lives."*[21]

MY STORY OF PURPOSE CONFUSION

I was about ready to graduate high school when I remember contemplating the big question, "What am I going to do with my life?" I was self-aware enough to know that I enjoyed doing certain things, like communicating and helping families.

I figured I could become a family counselor and motivational speaker, like a Tony Robbins for families. I mean hey, writing best-selling books and making six figures while speaking to thousands of eager followers in sold-out venues sounded alright to me!

But that was my personal pursuit, not necessarily God's purpose. Nevertheless, I went off to Bible school and decided to become the Church-world version of Tony Robbins and have a "world-wide traveling ministry." All I needed was to have two or three awesome messages, preach them all around the globe, and Boom! I would become Christian-famous!

Now it all sounds so shallow. And it was. But to be honest, don't all personal pursuits seem shallow when you take a closer look? Personal dreams are almost all based on self-centered goals, even when they are cloaked in a Christian disguise (a.k.a., the Church-world Tony Robbins!) or basted with a Christian flavor.

So, I went to Bible College. Fast forward a little, now. I'm falling in love with a beautiful girl; she loves to travel, wants to do some missions. I'm getting excited about the possibility of life with her. I thought I had life all figured out.

But in my final year of school, something began to change in me. God started rearranging the pursuits of my heart. He started speaking to me about His purpose for my life. In fact, every time I heard the words "pastor" and "local church" my heart beat a little faster and those words echoed in my mind for a solid thirty seconds. I soon got the impression God was trying to tell me something, but I wasn't sure I really wanted to know what it was.

Finally, I surrendered and asked God what He was saying. Over the course of a few days, He spoke to me. *"Son, your thoughts aren't really My thoughts on this subject. I've got some different thoughts than you have about your purpose,"* He seemed to say. He also gave me these words: *Husband. Father. Pastor/Communicator.* God was rearranging my pursuit to align with His purpose. Of all the things I was excited about before (traveling, being a famous "Tony Robbins" figure, missions, etc.), the one thing I got right was the girl! For that, I'm beyond grateful!!

Fast forward again. We're now living in North Carolina, we're married, we have one child, and our second one is on the way! We're in ministry in a local church. Life is very full.

I start getting confused about my life's purpose with God, again. All the things I felt I was to accomplish were now completed, or so I thought. I began to wonder, *"Is my life over? Is God done with me? God, what do I do next?"*

God clearly and lovingly (as He always does) told me that those three Words He gave me were not *activities to accomplish and check off a to-do list*, but rather *filters or pathways of purpose that would guide me throughout my entire life.* The words "husband, father, and pastor/communicator" were His purposes, and were to serve as guides for how to live my life.

As a pastor/communicator, I was supposed to live my life communicating the gospel of Jesus with creativity and passion. It wasn't about the job of being a senior pastor or being a youth pastor or being a kid's pastor or being an associate pastor. Whatever the job, role or context, I was to creatively communicate the Gospel.

The same was true about the word husband. It wasn't about just being the best husband I knew how to be; although that is a God-honoring pursuit and passion. But It also meant I was to live my life so committed to the church and to her people that I would love them sacrificially, like a husband loves his wife; lovingly serving them, again and again.

And finally, being a dad is indeed one of the greatest joys I have in life. The opportunity to create a Godly legacy is one I don't take for granted. It certainly is not just another activity to check off. Being a father is my heart's posture not only with my children, but also with the church. I am to lead others like a father would lead his family lovingly, tenderly caring for them, looking out for them, training them. I am not to be consumed with being an important leader, but rather with being like a father, helping them reach their full potential and believing in them even when they don't believe in themselves.

I truly believe purpose is a pathway on which we walk, not a destination we arrive at. Don't restrict God's purpose to specific tasks you can check off your list. Purpose is bigger than that. God's purpose is more of a pathway or direction that we walk. We can't afford to be confused about our purpose. God wants to give you clarity of purpose as a gift, and help you walk a path of significance. But the journey of significance starts with surrender of self-centered pursuits.

When it comes to your own life, *who you are becoming is more important than what you do as a career.* Your character and purpose must be shaped by God's character and purpose. We are most alive and become the truest versions of ourselves when we are being transformed into the image of Christ,[22] for His good works.[23] As you read God's Word, it will begin to shift your heart and mind toward God's purposes. Then you will know where to aim your life, finding the point to it all.

LASER FOCUSED

I was watching some YouTube videos recently about what a laser can do. Some Lasers are small enough to use in a slide presentation, others are so powerful that they are military weapons. Some lasers are used to help renew energy and help in an industrial arena. Some lasers are so focused and so intense that they can cause devastating damage, while others can be used to perform surgery and aid healing.

What gives a laser its power? The power of a laser is found in the focus of its energy. This focused, intense light can be used for good or to cause pain. I'm sure you're already tracking me. Our light, our energies, can be focused for good or evil as well.

What if we took the light of Christ, allowed our lives to focus on heavenly purposes and aligned with God-honoring priorities, what good could we do? What if we got so laser-focused in our faith, that we became part of Christ's healing process, bringing hope and restoration to our own and others' broken and disjointed souls?

What if we stop chasing the things that we think are going to satisfy our lives and instead go to the Creator of the world and ask, "God, what do you want to satisfy me with? What do you want to do in me? What do you want to do through me?"

I wonder if our willingness to lay down our own personal pursuits and preferences could begin to heal our relationships? What if the culture around us would once again see a picture of God's covenant love through our marriages?

Much could be restored, and many of God's promises would be received, if we'd just focus our lives on God's ways, acknowledging that His ways are better than ours. His priorities are much more impactful than our preferences.

I say let's try it and live today God's way! Before we say "yes" to anything, before we go on about our regular routines, or even before we make out our "to-do" list today, let's pause and ask God if He wants us to do it. Let's acknowledge Him in ALL our ways and see what path we end up taking.

I bet if we do this every day, we will accomplish more by doing less.

He will bring rain that will satisfy. His Word will not return void. And we'll eat and feast on the things that genuinely satisfy us in life.

Why? Because we will be living with a purpose shaped through priorities that come from being laser-focused on Him.

[6] Unity with Humility

The most important matters of our lives are affected by the thoughts that we think, and we can transform our mindset by changing our thoughts.

One Biblical mindset that is counter-cultural is this idea: pursue unity with humility!
Why should we pursue unity with humility?

1 Corinthians 1:10 says. *"I appeal to you, brothers and sisters, in the name of our Lord Jesus Christ, that all of you agree with one another in what you say and that there be no divisions among you, but that you be perfectly united in mind and thought."*

In other words, your mindset affects your ability to walk in humility and unity with others.

You cannot have unity in any relationship without pre-deciding to walk in humility. If we don't pre-decide to have a mindset of humility, we become reactionary to the emotions of the moment, both our emotions and the emotions of others. When we are reactionary instead of

You cannot have **unity** in any relationship without pre-deciding to walk in **humility**.

#MindsetMattersBook

humble, we will have many negative effects on our families, organizations, and relationships.

UNITY IS NOT CONFORMITY

What is unity? Unity is not conformity. Unity doesn't mean we all look, act, and talk robotically, like programmed artificial intelligence. Unity, when rooted in God's love, does not remove individual expressions. Nor is it even full agreement on every detail.

In truth, 100% agreement isn't always possible. That's why humility is critical. You can disagree and not be disagreeable.

Now, just to be clear, unity does occur when you walk in agreement. And it's a great feeling to go in the same direction as someone else. There is tremendous power when we pray with each other in unity and stay in God's Word as we walk forward in agreement together.

But sometimes we come to a crossroads where we don't see eye-to-eye on certain things. My wife and I don't always agree on every decision for our kids. And you may not always agree with every decision your company makes. A decision made by your local government might not be how you would've handled things. Or a choice your parents pass along to you might not be your thing. It's at these moments that you hit the crossroads of disagreement.

The only way to continue moving in unity with others when this happens, continuing in the same direction and on the same path, is if somebody decides to submit. Then you can walk together in the same direction. Therefore, humility is required. To submit to one another, humility is a must.

Walking in submission to another person in your life or community means allowing them to take the lead while you voluntarily step into a supporting role. This is one of the most excellent demonstrations of humility. Choosing submission is a God-honoring act.

It was Rupertus Meldenius, a German theologian in the early seventeenth century, who said, "In essentials, unity, in non-essentials, liberty, and in all things, charity."[24] In other words, we're going to act out love no matter the scenario. Love is the primary force that helps us submit at the crossroads, prioritizing the relationship over fighting to be "right" in an argument.

DIVISIONS AND DENOMINATIONS

Let's review 1 Corinthians 1:10 again. *Listen carefully.*
"I appeal to you, brothers and sisters, in the name of our Lord Jesus Christ, that all of you agree with one another in what you say and that there be no divisions among you, but that you be perfectly united in mind and thought."

What is Paul saying? Remember, He was writing to Christians.

First, let me clarify what I DON'T think Paul is trying to say.
- He is not saying you shouldn't have denominations.
- He is not saying you shouldn't have a kid's department, worship department, or outreach department in your church.
- He is not saying you shouldn't have any sort of organization within a church.
- He is not saying that all churches should be the same and do everything together.

So, what IS Paul saying?

Paul is calling for those who love Jesus to choose unity of "mind and thought." Based on this passage, Paul would be wholly against a spirit of divisiveness that results in church splits over petty issues, community competition between denominations, or power-plays and political jockeying within churches. Another thing to consider is that the prefix "di" used in the word "division" means "two"; therefore, division, by definition, means "multiple visions." That makes sense, doesn't it? Division always occurs when there are competing visions for the purpose and outcome of a situation. No relationship can remain stable when it has split vision.

Let's look at another cultural institution, the university. Every college or university offers several majors to explore, all in the name of getting a higher education. There may be multiple majors and departments, but the overall vision is to provide a quality education. Similarly, the "capital C"

Church has many different expressions but one overall vision. In colleges, we recognize that different schools are best suited for different types of students. In the same way, different churches in a community – even though they are all committed to the same gospel of Jesus Christ – are best suited for different types of believers.

I genuinely believe that each healthy church is distinct and different in their strategy or approach to accomplishing our shared mission in spreading the gospel. Any church that preaches Jesus and points people to a vibrant faith-relationship with God is okay by me! It takes different types of churches to reach different types of people.

Undoubtedly, even among similar churches, every individual congregation has its own uniqueness. When it comes to essentials, we want and need to have unity. But in other things that really are non- essential, let's just celebrate those differences and have a thoughtful dialogue instead of a fight.

In the county where I pastor, there are over 50 different churches. We only have around fourteen thousand people in the whole county. Is our church competing with the other 49 churches? No, we're not. I understand that all the churches are not the same. But I am really okay with it. Why? Because our church's mission is to reach people that nobody else is reaching. If we're going to reach people that nobody is reaching, then obviously, we must do things differently! Our church will never compromise the essential truths of scripture, but our methods will need to be different.

I didn't always think like this. There was a time when my mindset was quite legalistic and lacked humility. I never thought of the variety of denominations in Christianity as a positive thing, but instead viewed other churches as competitors. Then my pastor, Dale Jenkins, helped reshape my mindset along these lines. He himself embodied humility and celebrated so many various types of churches. After spending over nine years serving on his staff, my mindset was re-shaped by Pastor Dale's welcoming attitude toward other expressions of Christ's body.

UNITY IS TRAVELING IN THE SAME DIRECTION

Why is this change of mindset important? Because Unity is the key to experiencing God's blessing, goodness and presence. The presence of God is the very thing that propels us forward in life.

> *Psalms 133:1-3 says,*
> *"How good and pleasant it is for brothers and sisters to dwell together in unity. It is like precious oil poured on the head, running down on the beard, running down on Aaron's beard, down on the collar of his robe. It is as if the dew of Hermon were falling on Mount Zion. For there, the Lord bestows his blessing, even life forevermore."*

Where there is unity, the presence of God is evident. The opposite is also true; where there is no unity; the presence of God cannot reside. This is a problem because the very thing that makes a church or an individual life-giving is the presence of God at work in them. Without His presence, the church is no different than a social club. But with His presence, everything changes. One encounter with the presence of God can change any life!

Deciding to walk together in unity with humility gives God permission to keep His promise. Psalm 133:3 tells us that it is there (brothers living in unity) that the Lord bestows His blessing.

Exactly what is God's blessing? God's blessing is not merely getting more "stuff." God's blessing is the promise of His Spirit and His goodness that manifests itself in so many tangible ways. The goodness of God is real joy; it's a peace that goes beyond our understanding; it's patience and a deep realization of His unfailing and unchanging love.

As I look back over recent years and the landscape of American Christianity, I must say that there has been a firestorm of political and moral issues that have created heated divides among Christians, and beyond the church, in our nation and in our local communities as well.

Topics like Planned Parenthood, which restrooms people can use, equality of the genders, equality of pay, and even gender identity have created sharp divides. Social media movements with causes like Black Lives Matter, Police

Mindset *Matters*

Lives Matter and All Lives Matter, have all given online opportunities for the evils in our hearts to be on full display.

Each of these causes has merit and is a heavy-weight topic with valuable people supporting each side. Sprinkle in this mix controversies such as should believers drink alcohol? Should we shop at Target? Are medicines and vaccines better than all-natural oils and other organic ways to care for our children's health?

Oh, and who can forget about the infamous "color of a coffee cup" controversy? Remember when one popular coffee company at Christmas time, a couple of years ago, decided not to use red cups that year? Somehow that led many to believe that the coffee company was refusing to celebrate Christmas and was disrespecting Christians and therefore we should all boycott said coffee company!

The crazy thing is, not all issues are so silly. On many of these issues, I find that I might agree with certain talking points on both sides and could even find Scriptures to back them up! But the problem is, when we get sidelined into arguments like these, we can't see the forest for the trees.

When we are argumentative, nobody can hear our message about Jesus anymore because of our madness. Some turn social media into a megaphone, and use it like the new "street corner," shouting and waving signs at every passerby. But would you listen to someone yelling at you through a megaphone on the street? In the same way, nobody is going to listen to us yelling at them and arguing through an online "megaphone."

I'm not saying that we shouldn't have convictions in our lives, or evaluate culture based on them.

But what I am saying is that those convictions must be expressed with humility, and ways that people can hear us. Otherwise our words will only stir more strife instead of delivering clarity. Expressing our convictions with humility in ways that create clarity and healing matters a lot.

"But, Pastor, we are just defending our faith; after all, Christianity is under attack," some say.

But since when did God say that Christianity won't be threatened? Or tell us that He needs our help to defend His Church?

Never. But He did say He would build His Church, and hell itself can't come against it.[25] We cannot afford to lose our unity because of fear that trials or social pressure may mount.

MEAT AND IDOLS

In Paul's day, a central controversy was the subject of meat and idols. The argument wasn't really within the larger culture; it was a controversy between church-folk.

The big beef was that people were eating meat that had been previously offered to idols. This was considered taboo by the former pagans, to say the least.

Today such a practice would be like a "guilt by association" verdict. You can't shop at Store X, because Store X supports organizations that are contrary to Biblical morality. Therefore, by shopping at Store X, you don't have Biblical morality. Or, you can't eat at restaurants that have a bar in them, or at least if you do, you can't sit at the bar, even if you're not drinking alcohol! Someone might catch you and assume you're getting drunk, and thus, you ruin your "witness."

But enough re-lived trauma from my life. Back to Paul.

> *"Accept ones whose faith is weak, without quarreling over disputable matters. One person's faith allows them to eat anything but another whose faith is weak, eat only vegetables organic all the way. The one who eats everything must not treat with contempt the one who does not, and the one who does not eat everything must not judge the one who does, for God has accepted them. One person considers one day more sacred than another, and another considers every day to be exactly alike. Each one of them should be fully convinced in their own mind. Whoever regards one day as special does so to the Lord, and whoever eats meat does so to the Lord, for they both give thanks to God." (Rom. 14:1-6)*

Paul is talking about amoral things that are not an issue of sin. Some behaviors or practices are beneficial, and some are not beneficial, based on everyone's preferences or needs, but they are not moral choices. Individuals might choose an alternative healthcare approach or have a preference to home-educate versus using the public school system. Some people sense God asking them to live a certain way, perhaps abstaining from a particular food or activity, but that doesn't mean everyone has to duplicate their choices.

RELATIONSHIPS WITH PEOPLE MATTER MORE.

Do you value being right in an argument more than being in right relationship? Does your "freedom" to drink alcohol (without getting drunk) matter more to you than being with a friend who is a recovering addict and can't be around you at all if alcohol is present?

Here's the core of everything that we're talking about today: relationships matter. Relationships matter to God because people matter to God. God did not say that you must fight for the truth. He said to live out the truth. But He didn't say "I'm going to give you the superpower to win every argument in the name of Truth and be superior to everyone else in your morality."

I believe there is room in scripture for you to be on one side of an idea or topic, while somebody else thinks differently than you. Both people will still go to heaven. And both still are considered believers; both still are capable of walking in unity with humility.

It's super easy to be against something. It takes much more effort to be for something. Our tendency as believers is to see something we don't agree with, or just don't like, and begin to blow it up on Facebook. Posting one meme after another, we work ourselves into a frenzy over things that maybe, just maybe, aren't such a big deal. Nobody is going to heaven because they drink coffee from a red cup versus a white paper cup at Christmas. Your salvation is not on such thin ice that if you dance at a wedding you will burn in hell.

If the convictions you're defending honor God, good. But if the real issue is just that you want to be "right" and better than others, then please stop. Because the point is to bring honor and glory to God, not to stand up to others and say, "I was right, and you were wrong."

You cannot earn right-standing with God, and your behavior does not determine your salvation. Your belief in Jesus determines your salvation.

Paul takes it a step further in Romans 14:13-22:
> *"Instead, make up your mind not to put any stumbling block or obstacle in the way of a brother or sister. I am convinced, being fully persuaded in the Lord Jesus, that nothing is unclean in itself. But if anyone regards something as unclean, then for that person it is unclean. If your brother or sister is distressed because of what you eat, you are no*

longer acting in love. Do not by your eating destroy someone for whom Christ died. Therefore, do not let what you know is good to be spoken of as evil. For the kingdom of God is not a matter of eating and drinking, but of righteousness, peace, and joy in the Holy Spirit, because anyone who serves Christ in this way is pleasing to God and receives human approval. Let us, therefore, make every effort to do what leads to peace and to mutual edification. Do not destroy the work of God for the sake of food. All food is clean, but it is wrong for a person to eat anything that causes someone else to stumble. It is better not to eat meat or drink wine or to do anything else that will cause your brother or sister to fall. So, whatever you believe about these things keep between yourself and God. Blessed is the one who does not condemn himself by what he approves."

Why so much concern about these issues? Because your mindset matters!

Make up your mind not to put any stumbling block or obstacle in the way of a brother or sister. Just don't do it! Don't put a stumbling block in front of them. Is it possible that our very judgmentalism and moralism, on non-Biblical issues, creates stumbling blocks so massive that others cannot get past them to see Jesus?

My pastor once said, "As long as we (believers) sit in the judgment seat, Christ can't occupy that seat.

If I'm sitting in a seat to judge somebody, even if it seems like I am there for a good reason, Christ can't sit in that seat, too."

I don't know about you, but I would much prefer that the perfect, Righteous One is sitting in that seat. He is entirely merciful yet perfectly just, all at the same time. Jesus is the judge; I am not.

PERSONAL VS. BIBLICAL

Personal convictions are not the same as Biblical commands. I think this is where Philippians 2:12 comes into play:

> *"Therefore, my dear friends, as you have always obeyed—not only in my presence but now much more in my absence—continue to work out your salvation with fear and trembling."*

The "fear and trembling" mentioned here is not because we need to be afraid that one wrong deed will eliminate our salvation, but rather, that we must carefully approach our relationship with God. We must live honestly before God and allow His Spirit to lead us in each stage of life.

Many of our personal convictions are not biblical commands. We must respectfully and practically be sensitive to the uniqueness of each person and the journey God has for them.

It didn't matter what time I met with God in the past. I used to have my devotions at night. But one day, God told me He wanted me to get up and start my day with Him. So, for me, doing devotions in the morning is a personal standard God called me to embrace. However, it would be foolish and arrogant to assume that morning devotions are the BEST way for everyone to live. To be honest, the best time for you to do your devotions is when you're at your best!

DIFFERENT SEASONS

For some people it is perfectly okay for them to go to a buffet and indulge, eating all they want, and it doesn't affect their weight one bit. But not all of us are blessed with such digestive capacity. Most of us must regulate and count our carbs, proteins, or sugars. Sure, there are specific dietary baselines we all need to adhere to for optimum health, but my kid's metabolism, for example, permits them to eat large amounts of foods that my metabolism just can't process at that rate anymore!

In the same way, spiritually, each of us must ask the Holy Spirit to lead us in a way that keeps us on track with what is beneficial for our souls; with what recharges our spirit. We must judge and discern those things and make decisions based on what is right according to God's Word.

There are specific standards that I'm living by because I know God Himself is judging me as a teacher of the Word more strictly. According to James 3:1, He says teachers will be judged more strictly. Whereas you are not responsible for what I teach every Sunday, I will stand before God and give an account for those things. So, my week is structured, in a rather stringent way, around ensuring I get plenty of study and prayer time for the messages I teach.

Different seasons require different standards. Your children may love cola beverages and drink them daily. We try and limit the amount of cola our kids drink. Do we limit it because it's a sin? No! We limit it because they cannot control themselves with sugar.
Do Christians need convictions? Yes! But we cannot afford to confuse our personal convictions with Biblical commands.

Is there evil in our world? You bet. Do we need to overcome evil by doing good? Yes. But too often what we do instead is to attempt to overcome evil with a Facebook meme or a Twitter Truth-spat. Overcoming evil with good depends on how you live your life. It is your testimony and your pursuit of Jesus that demonstrate the goodness of God, not the memes you share online.

If you and I focus our attention on developing a healthy relationship with God, our lives will be attractive to others. We cannot spend so much time inspecting other people's fruit that we stop abiding in Christ and bearing fruit ourselves.

Every time we're told to correct sinful behavior in Scripture, we're told to do so within the context of relationships. This implies that if I don't have a personal

We cannot spend so much time **inspecting** other people's fruit that we stop **abiding in Christ** and bearing fruit ourselves.

#MindsetMattersBook

relationship with someone, it is my responsibility to pray for them, not to correct or confront them.

"But pastor, if we don't use our freedom of speech, if we don't stand up, if we don't ... (etc.) ... " and on and on it goes.

I think sometimes we use the term "freedom of speech" as an excuse to be undisciplined with our words. And that's precisely what Paul addressed in Romans when he instructs us that it's better to stay quiet and keep disagreements between yourselves.

You may have the freedom to speak, but you also have the freedom *not* to speak. The ability to restrain from speaking is wisdom, and an act of humility.

CULTIVATING HUMILITY

Humility is not always natural, but you can develop it. We can grow in our humility. Allow me to offer a few ideas on cultivating humility in our lives.

1. Repent often.

Do you know what the Word repentance means? It doesn't mean to cry out at an altar or to confess all your sins. Here's what repentance means: to change your mindset so that it is aligned with God's mindset and move in a different direction with your life.

Biblical repentance is a changing of your mind; that's why your mindset matters! Your behavior will follow your mindset.

2. Apologize quickly.

If we want to pursue unity in relationships, we need to be willing to admit we did wrong or overstepped our boundaries. Saying "sorry" is not an apology; it's not actually an admission that you did anything wrong. These six words will save almost every relationship: "I. Was. Wrong. Please. Forgive. Me." Go ahead, give these words a try this week.

3. Bow before God.

When was the last time you got on your knees in worship to the Lord? When was the last time you got on your knees in prayer? When was the last time you recognized that God's presence had come into the room and rather than standing, you bowed before the Lord? Bowing down is a posture of the humble and expresses our submission to God.

4. Ask more questions.

There's a difference between asking a question and questioning something. One seeks to foster a relationship and understand. The other looks to criticize, often looking down on the person or idea we are questioning. Become a person who is good at asking the type of questions that foster relationships. Make it your goal to foster the relationship instead of winning the debate.

5. Pray more than you post.

Pray more than you post on social media! Saying you're praying for somebody in a post is not the same thing as praying for somebody. Complaining to a friend is not the same as praying about it. What if it is our lack of our humility and true commitment to prayer that has created the undercurrent of division in our world today?

PURSUE HUMILITY

We must have the mindset that pursues unity with humility! Why? Because we need God's grace.

"For God resists the proud but releases His grace to the humble." (1 Pet. 5:5)

I don't want to live my life without God's grace; His saving grace, His forgiving grace, or His restoring grace. His power or grace helps us overcome the situations and the difficulties that we face in life.

I especially don't want to miss out on His grace because I was too busy trying to be right in my own eyes! That's called self-righteousness. I want to be truly right before God. I want to live in right relationship with other people, and that requires me to pursue unity with a high dose of humility. I want to live and cultivate the humble life.

Augustine of Hippo said it like this, "If you believe whatever you like in the Gospel and reject what you don't like, It's not the gospel that you believe, but it's yourself that you believe."[26]

So, let's walk in humility. Let's stride toward unity and allow Jesus to be the LORD and the just judge. Let's not confuse personal convictions with Biblical commands. And let's value the relationship more than being right in an argument. Then our lives will truly experience God's blessing and we will see His goodness for ourselves!

[7] Expectation + Gratitude

One of the first skills a parent must master is the art of giving your children hope without making a promise. There is a fine line between crushing their hearts and making promises that break you. You see, a child remembers what you promise them. To some children, even a reliable "maybe" is all the promise they need. When a child hears you promise you'll do something for them, no amount of distraction or linguistic aerobics can convince them you didn't guarantee it if their mind is set that you gave a promise.

I am thankful we serve a God who not only keeps His promises but makes sure the promise is evident when He does make one. When God follows through for us on a promise, our faith expectations of Him are rewarded and we can respond with tremendous gratitude.

God made some significant promises to the Israelites. One worth pointing out is in the book of Deuteronomy.

> *"For the Lord your God is bringing you into a good land, a land of brooks of water, of fountains and springs that flow out of valleys and hills; a land of wheat and barley, of vines*

and fig trees and pomegranates, a land of olive oil and honey; a land in which you will eat bread without scarcity, in which you will lack nothing; a land whose stones are iron and out of whose hills you can dig copper. When you have eaten and are full, then you shall bless the Lord your God for the good land which He has given you.

Beware that you do not forget the Lord your God by not keeping His commandments, His judgments, and His statutes which I command you today, lest—when you have eaten and are full, and have built beautiful houses and dwell in them; and when your herds and your flocks multiply, and your silver and your gold are multiplied, and all that you have is multiplied; when your heart is lifted up, and you forget the Lord your God who brought you out of the land of Egypt, from the house of bondage; who led you through that great and terrible wilderness, in which were fiery serpents and scorpions and thirsty land where there was no water; who brought water for you out of the flinty rock; who fed you in the wilderness with manna, which your fathers did not know, that He might humble you and that He might test you, to do you good in the end—then you say in your heart, 'My power and the might of my hand have gained me this wealth.'

And you shall remember the Lord your God, for it is He who gives you the power to get wealth, that He may establish His covenant which He swore to your fathers, as it is this day."
(Deut. 8:7-18)

Expectation + Gratitude

God is indeed a God of abundance. God didn't leave anything unclear. He wanted the Israelites to have an expectation that He would care for them in every way. And care for them He did!
I can imagine the first time the Israelites saw all the pomegranates and all the rivers, the abundance of olive oil and honey, or realized that they had all the bread they could possibly want to eat for the first time in a generation, they were filled with joy! I am sure their joy and gratitude blessed God's heart. As a parent you know that nothing is quite as rewarding as seeing your child respond with authentic and joyous gratitude because you kept your promise to them, just as you said you would.

In 2016 we moved from North Carolina to Kansas. Our two oldest kids started a brand-new school in the middle of the school year. One of the things we wanted to do was make it a memorable time and make attending the new school something they looked forward to attending. We wanted to make sure they had something positive to look forward to each week as they faced the challenges of starting a new school, making new friends, and adjusting to a whole different environment.

To give them at least one positive event to look forward to each week, regardless of what was happening at school, we started treating our kids to Dairy Queen every Thursday for an after-school snack. They loved it! It got to the point, they would run to the car, fling the doors open, and exclaim, "Dad, it's DQ Thursday!!!!!" All the teachers in the car pick-up line knew about it, their friends heard about it, and our kids were genuinely giddy with their expectations for Thursdays. We made them a promise, we kept it, and they had full confidence that we'd not back down.

God is a better parent than you and me, and He has given us many promises to help get us through our hard times, too. According to scripture, all of God's promises are trustworthy! 2 Corinthians 1:20 says, *"For all the promises of God in Him are Yes, and in Him Amen, to the glory of God through us."*

Faith expectations are an engine that drives our mindset to believe for what we don't yet have. That's why verses like 2 Corinthians 1:20 are such great verses to install into the memory banks of our minds. When doubt creeps in, we need to be able to stay resolute that our God keeps His promises and remain as confident as a child when a faithful parent makes a promise.

Expectation and entitlement are two very different things, however. Without gratitude, our faith-based expectations can slip into the danger zone of feeling we are entitled to something from God. An entitlement, as defined by Merriam Webster, is a "belief that one is deserving of or entitled to certain privileges."[27] Such an "entitlement" is a sense of privilege; a desire that demands to be met because we somehow feel we "deserve" it. A faith expectation, conversely, is based not on our merit but on the promise giver's reliability.

That is why it stands to reason that God warned Israel not to forget that it was Him who gave them the power to make wealth and who provided for them.[28] The remedy to their potential sense of entitlement was gratitude. Gratitude guards against the contaminant of pride by reminding us to thank the One who made and kept the promise. To say it simply, gratitude is the remedy to an entitled heart.

REJOICE ALWAYS

It was early 2018 when I noticed my kids were – well, how shall we say it – perfecting the "art of complaining." In fact, their complaining suddenly increased exponentially. Here we were, living in a beautiful gift-from-God home in Kansas, we had successfully transitioned our lives from North Carolina to Kansas, and life was good! But instead of gratitude, it seemed my kids had some short-term memory loss. The kids had food, clothes, and were fresh off from a great Christmas! Yet the complaining got so bad that I was teetering between wanting to bring Godly instruction into their lives vs. burning every one of their new toys out of fatherly indignation!

So finally, I sat them all down and said, "We are going to do devotions this week as a family." Every night the week after Christmas we got together, turned off all the iPads, games, and TV shows, and gathered in the living room on our super comfy couches. We turned to Philippians 4:4, which says, "Rejoice in the Lord always, and again I say rejoice," and I taught this verse to them over and over, every single night. We memorized it together as a family.

Gratitude
is the remedy to an entitled heart.

#MindsetMattersBook

Now, my kids were in the younger elementary age range at this time, and, being a former children's pastor, I made sure to make this time fun, including hand motions to help them memorize the verse.

This focused teaching on gratitude paid off! It turned out that I was helping my kids recalibrate their minds. I wanted them to remember that it is the Lord who blesses us, and it is the Lord who provides for us. He takes care of us, and our appropriate response is to be grateful. My kids needed their mind (and attitude) adjusted to reflect those truths. Gratitude recalibrates our mindset.

Complaining has a way of making us forget the source of our blessings. We slip into a mode of entitlement and lose sight of God's handiwork. We start taking for granted the big and small ways that God is at work.

Maybe you can relate to this. Perhaps it's time to recalibrate your heart and refresh your mindset by choosing to rejoice, always. Ask the Holy Spirit to stop you, mid-complaint!

I believe every promise from God is a seed that goes into the soil of our hearts.[29] If we're not careful, our complaining will contaminate the soil itself. No matter what it is that God has promised, it cannot grow fruit in our lives if our constant complaining is choking the life right out of the seed. Like Roundup® poisons and quickly kills green grass, complaining poisons the soil of our hearts.

Psalms 77:12-14, says, *"I will consider all your works and meditate on all your mighty deeds. Your ways, God, are holy. What God is as great as our God? You are the God who performs miracles; you display your power among the peoples."*

I love that Psalm. Meditating on God's mighty deeds, past and present, helps keep our minds in a place of gratitude and praise. The more we focus on what God has done previously, the more promptly we realize what He is doing presently. Gratitude keeps our faith, or expectations, from being sabotaged.

DISCOLORED VISION

One of our first winters in Kansas was forecast to be quite brutal. Yet, for a long stretch, we experienced the opposite – some abnormally warm weather. In fact, the weather was wonderful! On one of those nice days I decided to go for a run.

I took off for a run near our community college, which has a track that winds around a mini lake. About a mile and a half into my run, about the halfway point for me, I saw three or four people out fishing on the lake. It seemed as if they were relaxing and enjoying themselves so much. At that very same moment I was literally sweating and beginning to get tired. Suddenly, I found myself thinking, *"I wish I was fishing right now!"*

Now, I must give a quick side-note here. I don't fish. Honestly. I don't even own a fishing pole. But for whatever reason, that day I started getting jealous! The more I compared the relaxation of those people fishing to my labored breathing from running, the more frustrated I became.

"Man, these people are just lazing around fishing. This is ridiculous. I hate them all. I'm out here running and sweating..." Suddenly God interrupted my thoughts, mid-complaint."Whoa, Whoa, Whoa! Who chose to go run?" He seemed to ask me.

"That's beside the point, Lord, we're not talking about me, we're talking about them!" I responded. Then the Lord lovingly gave me a different perspective.

"Listen, son, some of the people fishing aren't even catching any fish, but ALL of the people exercising are getting their exercise." My complaining was stopped in its tracks. The simple truth of it made me smile. All at once, I was both encouraged and convicted!

Our negative perspective about our life or the season of life we are in discolors our vision. In fact, I would go so far as to say that anytime we compare and complain, our view will be skewed.

Some people say that the grass is always greener on the other side of the fence, but one gentleman said it like this: "The grass is always greener over the septic tank!" Often, we convince ourselves something (really anything) is better than our current situation. Yet when we chase after that fantasy which was spawned by jealous comparisons, we find ourselves even more disappointed, realizing that what we complained about was not that bad after all! We need to shift our mindset away from comparison because it always leads us to complaining and disappointment.

NOT YET

There is a tension that exists between expectation and gratitude. These seem to be opposites of each other, but they are, instead, truly complementary.

Having faith-based expectations moves us forward toward goals, while gratitude and thankfulness help us acknowledge the good in today. Even if things are not yet perfect, we have made progress and are grateful that we are not where we used to be. This tension between our expectation that things could be better, coupled with our gratitude for how far we've come, helps to build strength in us. It helps us make peace with the fact that though we are not yet where we want to be in our faith, we are, nevertheless, *on the way.*

Expectation is the hope and faith we hold onto. It is the clear picture of who we want to become one day. Expectation is the goal we want to achieve. Expectation creates an internal hope or motivation to improve our lives, to move past disappointments, and to reach for what's next. Faith-based expectation helps us visualize the destination we are navigating toward.

Expectation gives positive vision to the **future.**

#MindsetMattersBook

This mindset of expectation balanced with gratitude keeps us from becoming complacent or entitled. One of the clearest indicators that someone has lost their vision of expectation and habit of gratitude is when they revert to a poverty mindset or a victim mentality.

A poverty mindset is based on a core belief that "scarcity" rules our lives and interactions, and even controls our expectations. For example, a poverty mindset tells us that there is never enough to go around, we should never spend any money; we must accept the fact that our opportunities are quite limited. Scarcity pounds into us a fear that any goodness or success we do achieve won't last; that all "risk" is detrimentally dangerous; and the only path to success in life is to try to go unnoticed, stay in the back, keep quiet, and generally "play it safe." Unfortunately, the lifestyle that springs up from this poverty mindset is *anything but safe.*

It is the poverty mindset that causes us to hoard unusable spare parts, because we fear we might need one someday and won't have them. So, we stockpile 7,000 spare bolts in a garage. Or, we might have an opportunity to put our name in for a promotion at work, but the poverty mindset has us convinced that our lack of education will disqualify us before we even try, so we never even apply. In some cases, divorcees won't remarry and go on with their lives because the poverty mindset fills them with fear that life without that alimony check each month won't work. Some people are tired of feeling alone while at church, but the poverty mindset has them too scared to reach out and join a small group.

A victim mindset is the first cousin to the poverty mindset and is equally discouraging. According to the victim mindset, all misfortune and lack of progress is somebody else's fault. The victim mindset reassures us that nothing is our fault, no matter what. The hand we were dealt was short-stacked and it is impossible for us to measure up to everyone else's standards. Maybe if we had a better boss, we would enjoy our work more and do a better job. Or maybe if we lived on the other side of town, or if our kid would get more playing time on the basketball team, we could finally get a little bit of respect. But no. It won't happen to us. When a poverty mindset and victim mindset gang up to root themselves in our hearts, they poison our sense of hope, faith, and anticipation in no time!

These cousin mindsets must be recognized and kicked out! They must be exchanged for a new mindset of personal responsibility in order to live in expectation of God's best along with gratitude for what goes right. The expectation/gratitude mindset is not a magic formula, but it is the path that allows us to move forward toward a life of God-honoring purpose.

I am not saying that if you just have a positive mindset, everything works out like magic. But I am saying that choosing a mindset of expectation and gratitude is the first step out of the pit of being stuck in your life. Expectation/gratitude creates a clear picture of hope in your mind that keeps you motivated when you feel the pressure building and want to give up. It's an antidote to limiting beliefs like " if you just had different parents your life would be better," "you can never trust things that are "too good to be true," or "you should never get your hopes up because nothing ever works out for you in the end."

These limiting beliefs are not what Jesus said. Jesus said that He came to give abundant life.[30] Proverbs 10:22 also says, "*the blessing of the Lord makes one rich, and **He adds no sorrow to it***" (emphasis added). We can confidently have an expectation that when God is at work in our lives, we have no shortage of joy, peace, love, even provision. The expectation of a prosperous and joyful life is founded on Jesus!

Expectation gives positive vision to the future. It helps develop eyes that see more than our current circumstances. You might be stuck in a really challenging situation right now, maybe even a crisis. Perhaps the difficulty you are facing resulted from decisions you made, or perhaps it was not your fault at all, but was somehow thrust upon you by things totally outside of your control. But no matter how you got here, once you are in crisis mode, the crisis is all you can think about.

But can I just encourage you to set your sights a little higher in order to get beyond the crisis?

Here's a little secret: when we are consumed with figuring out what went wrong, our eyes are looking down. When the eyes of our hearts are focused down at the problem instead of looking at God's best, we eventually feel less hopeful, stop caring and improving, and quit moving forward. We get stuck in the problem and start to settle for less than God's best. We compromise on our future and sell ourselves short. We may begin to live for immediate pleasure and decide to pay for it later. How many people do you know today who are still paying for poor choices they made years ago? That doesn't have to be you!

But as I mentioned earlier, if instead of looking down we purposely lift our eyes off the problem and set our sights high on God's promises and possibilities, we will begin to live with an element of expectation instead of dread. What will God do to deliver us? God is always close,[31] and He wants to make His goodness abound toward you![32] The quicker we look up to Him instead of down at our problems, the more easily we will rise up and become fully persuaded that God is more than able[33] to solve our mess!

This is an intentional shift in mindset, and you can choose it today. Start living in the excitement of higher expectations as you move onward and upward with your sights set on God!

What would your life look like if you started living with a mindset of expectation for your future, one that is full of faith? What if your vision of the future was created by an expectation based on the promises in God's Word? The first step of experiencing the abundant life Christ talked about is believing that God wants better things for your life and has an abundant life planned for you if you follow Him. I must caution you, though, that expectation without gratitude towards God will lead you to legalism. Life becomes very legalistic when you're trying to control an outcome by following the rules instead of walking in expectant faith in God, the One that has the power to produce those great end-results. Your highest expectations must be based on your relationship with God, and your faith in His ability. Otherwise you will end up trying to achieve your expectations in your own effort. Lofty expectations without gratitude and relationship with God always leads to legalism.

Gratitude matters. Gratitude insulates our heart from being offended, from comparing ourselves to others, and from legalism. If we can combine high expectations with gratitude, our hearts will be so insulated that when something happens in our life that just doesn't seem fair, we will start thanking God for what He's done for us rather than complaining and being envious.

Gratitude keeps us out of the weeds in the "that's not fair" mentality. It softens our heart and brightens our outlook.

Therefore, Paul encourages us in I Thessalonians 5:18 that we are to "*in all things, give thanks!*" We don't need to give thanks *for* everything - but *in* everything. For example, we don't give thanks *for* cancer, but we do give thanks *during* a cancer battle, even as we set our expectation toward healing. We don't have to give thanks *for* taxes, but we can give thanks *in* tax season for the many services that our taxes provide to our communities, even though our tax return isn't as much as we hoped it would be.

GIVE THANKS: THE ANTIDOTE TO "THAT'S NOT FAIR!"

Sibling rivalry is a real deal, right? The words "that's not fair" are uttered more amongst young siblings than perhaps in any other context. Anytime kids feel like they are getting the short end of the stick, they start comparing and complaining about each other. It exasperates us as parents when the kids do it, but the truth is, we still do it as adults. Complaining is often a "That's not fair!" moment for adults. When we start complaining, it poisons our joy and sucks the fun out of relationships. How can we break this habit?

Giving thanks is the antidote. In Psalms 136, we read an entire song instructing us to "Give thanks to the Lord."[34] Why? Simply because He is good. God is good, all the time, no matter what else is going on in our world. And when we speak words of gratitude to the Lord, it changes the content of our hearts, and it builds our faith.

Why is building our faith so important? Faith is important because all that God has to offer us – the blessings, and the promises – are received and activated through faith. Faith is like a muscle we need to develop through use, and gratitude is the exercise we use to strengthen that muscle. It takes both to live the abundant life.

THE MOMENTUM OF FAITH

There is a big difference between specific gratitude and general gratitude. Sometimes general appreciation can be passed off as insincere, just being polite. But when you get specific and descriptive with your gratitude, you open hearts and build stronger relationships. There is a big difference between telling someone that you appreciate them in a general way, versus telling someone the specific things about them that you really appreciate. Telling someone specific things you appreciate about them infuses your personal relationship with confidence and a sense of safety. It is always great to know that someone notices and appreciates you in certain specific ways.

It is the same in our relationship with God. It is good to thank Him in general, but if you want your relationship with God to be powerfully strengthened and full of new confidence, get specific with your gratitude toward Him! Make it your goal to write down three specific things you are grateful for about God each night. Then watch your faith grow stronger as a result!

Unfortunately, the flip side is also just as real. Constant complaining about the hand you've been dealt in life will weaken your relationship with God. Complaining has a way of repelling God's presence. Psalms tell us the pathway into God's presence is thanksgiving and praise.[35] This means that if we don't feel like God is near, it may be an indicator that we've been complaining more than we have been praising. We can flip the switch, though, and bring ourselves closer to Him again by simply choosing to give God praise and express our gratitude and thanksgiving.

God is more than able to do anything we need Him to do! Let's set our sights higher with expectations of God's goodness, based on His promises! Let's start dreaming God-size dreams for our families! Let's create an expectation for God to provide abundantly in our finances! Let's express our gratitude for His protection in the past and thank Him now for His care about our future!

Expectations like these activate our faith and open our eyes to see God's promises leading us to see God's promises come to life. When those promises come to life, specific gratitude is easy! That gratitude, expressed back to God, increases our confidence in Him and our expectation for the next hurdle! And so, a momentum of faith is set in motion.

In fact, moving forward into a victorious way of life depends on that very momentum of grateful faith. The mindset that builds up that momentum is the one we must maintain in order to keep being propelled toward God's best for our lives. Expectation and gratitude working together are the engine that keeps you from stalling out and helps you live victoriously with a strong and robust faith.

[8] Generosity + Stewardship

It was around 2007 when I first learned about Scott Harrison. He is the founder of an organization called Charity: Water, which is a non-profit helping fund clean water projects all over the globe, giving tribes and poor communities access to clean water.

I first learned about Charity: Water because a friend was giving up their birthday. You see, instead of asking for gifts or for us to attend their birthday party, my friend asked us to donate the dollar amount of their upcoming age to Charity: Water. It was a neat way to spark generosity and get the word out about a great cause.

Apparently, the idea for birthday-fundraising for Charity: Water began on September 9th, 2006, when Scott Harrison himself threw a big party to celebrate his 31st birthday and launch Charity: Water. He invited all his friends and charged $20 at the door. That night, he raised $15,000 for clean water projects.[36]

Soon, the idea caught on and many people were raising money for Charity: Water on their birthday, including actors, musicians, bloggers, and lawyers. Even children got involved!

Since then, all kinds of people have used their birthdays to make a difference for this group and others. This definitely left an impression on me.

Last time I checked, over $9M has already been raised for clean water through birthdays. The majority of that has come from average, unknown people who want to do something generous. A 25-year-old named Joey raised $5,050 for people in Africa.

A 30-year-old in Sydney raised $12,007. A 29-year-old girl in California just recently raised $32,398. It's staggering what simply encouraging generosity can accomplish for others! The generosity of Scott Harrison giving up his birthday so that others could have clean water has certainly left its mark on our world today.

Generosity always has a way of leaving its mark. Generosity positively impacts the person on the receiving end of the charity, but it also leaves a positive mark on the souls of those who do the giving or raise money, and those who witness the kindness as well.

This is the final mindset I want to look at together: a mindset of joyful generosity and faith-filled stewardship.

SET IT OR DRIFT FROM IT

"Set your minds on things above and not on earthly things." (Col. 3:2)

The command is direct: "Set your mind." In other words, you must anchor your thoughts in place, or they will drift. If you don't intentionally say, "Mind, this is what we're going to think about today," your mind will settle on various thought paths of its own.

The Bible teaches us to be good stewards of our mind and our money, and to be generous. But we don't naturally think the same way as the Bible instructs us to when it comes to our thinking about generosity and stewardship. That is why we must be intentional to set our minds in alignment with what Scripture teaches on this subject.

For some reason, it's easy to worry about money. I don't have to work hard at being stressed, worried, fearful, or even greedy when it comes to my bank account. Those characteristics seem to come somewhat naturally. I also find it unfortunately easy for my blood pressure to rise as I think about the bills and house repairs, and my kids' needs, or my future retirement.

But in order to not worry about money, I must set my mind and work hard at not worrying! I intentionally focus my mindset on things like trust, faith, risk, obedience, sacrifice, and generosity. Those wonderful thoughts do not come naturally when it comes to my bank account.

If I'm honest, my struggle with finding peace in this area reveals more about my heart than I'd like to admit.

TRACKER

Confession: I love buying things from Amazon. I love to hunt for things, to find nifty gadgets, to decide and order, and get just about anything I want in only two days. My Amazon treasure hunt goes something like this:

Search for it. Find it. Buy it. Track it. Receive it. Enjoy it. Then, rinse, repeat. Here we go again!

For those of you who are experienced online shoppers, I know you can relate to that process!

I must admit, the idea of tracking my purchases also intrigues me. You normally never care one bit about the weather in Utah. But come Christmas time, when that item you bought is stuck in a distribution warehouse in Utah, you may care about the weather in Utah enough to pray about it!

Why do we suddenly care so much? Our hearts get involved in these purchases. They have become little treasures to us.

Jesus said, "Where your treasure is, there your heart will also be." (Mt. 6:21) He was sure right! *Our hearts track with our money.*

> "Our **hearts** track with our **money**.

#MindsetMattersBook

JOYFUL GENEROSITY

We don't like to talk about money, especially in the church. But Jesus talked a lot about money. Why? He knew of this connection that money has to the heart. Jesus wants your heart, your whole heart. And Jesus tells us that we cannot serve both God and money.

Is this why so many people get upset when churches talk about money? Is it because the hearts of many church goers aren't really connected to the mission of Christ, but rather to serve their other god, money?

That question seems harsh, and I don't even like writing it. The thought makes me wince as well, probably because I want to downplay my own idol worship in this area.

But this is why tithing is so important. *Tithing is a systematic way to keep your heart pursuing the right things.* I would even take it as far as to say, tithing is commanded by God to protect our hearts from drifting into idol worship. In my life, and in the lives of many other people I know, the practice of tithing served as the training wheels in the process of developing a generous life.

If you have never read the book, "The Blessed Life" by Robert Morris, you need to! He also wrote another great book on the topic of stewardship entitled "Beyond Blessed." You should go buy both those books from Amazon right now! (Can you tell I'm a huge fan?)

LARGER

Generosity unlocks the heart toward God. Generosity also reveals to the world watching us that heaven is invading earth and is near. Generosity opens the door for the Gospel to be preached.

In fact, if God was not such a generous God, there would be no Gospel. The very center of the Gospel is that Jesus came as a gift. The coming of Jesus to the earth was the greatest act of generosity of all time. Just look at the first part of one of our most famous Scriptures, John 3:16:
*"For God so loved the world, **HE GAVE** His only son..."* (emphasis added).

Generosity is at the heart of the gospel and opens the door for the Gospel to be preached. Nothing better expresses the Gospel than acts of generosity. You're likely familiar with the phrase, "People don't care how much you know until they know how much you care." It's true. Often a single act of kindness displays such God-like generosity that it reinforces to people that God loves them. It's the Gospel in action.

Generosity points to the value of "honor" by showing honor to the recipients. I heard a story of somebody who decided that each week they would show other people how much they matter by doing something generous every "Make a Difference Monday." Every time they are in town on a Monday, this person goes through the drive-through of McDonald's and pays for somebody else's meal behind them. Not only is it a simple act of kindness that gives honor to others, it also serves as a powerful way to demonstrate God's love to someone else.

I love the verse in Proverbs 11:24, *"One person gives freely, yet gains even more; another withholds unduly but comes to poverty."*

Think about that. One person gives, but somehow while giving, gains more. But the other person keeps everything for himself, withholding unduly, and ends up coming to poverty! In other words, when somebody withholds and is stingy, somehow even what they have disappears! It's like there are holes in their pockets that they can't explain.

I love how The Message translation communicates this verse; it's one of my favorites. *"The world of the generous gets larger and larger, but the world of the stingy gets smaller and smaller."* (Prov. 11:24, The Message)

The "world of the generous gets larger and larger." Doesn't that just sound like God? It is the very nature of God to expand, grow and abound. People who live a God-honoring life understand that healthy things grow, expand, and abound. God wants your life, including your finances, to be ever-growing, ever-expanding, and ever-increasing.

When we set our minds on things of eternal importance, living generous lives and stewarding our resources in a God-honoring way, God brings an increase into our lives. This is God's desire for you! God wants your world to expand and not shrink.

There are generosity and stewardship principles in God's Word that produce fruit in our lives that we could not otherwise possess on our own. Let me describe to you what I mean.

When I think of a generous person whose world gets larger and larger, I think about someone who is full of joy. They're full of peace, they're content, and they're satisfied. Generous people are always increasing in humility, too, and they live responsibly. They're always growing in graciousness. These are the type of can-do people who are willing to dream!

Instead of being the first to point out the faults of others; Generous people are problem-solvers. In fact, generous people see possibilities where others find problems. Generous people are the crazy ones who are willing to believe that God means it when He tells us He can do more than we can ask or even imagine![37]

But now let me describe stingy people, who are just the opposite. Stingy people are selfish, discontent in life, and fearful of many things. They're oddly proud, judgmental, and anxious. Stingy folk are beyond pessimistic; not only is the glass half-empty, they are looking for who drank their water so they can beat them up! They are greedy and resentful. Every decision they make is based on a fear and poverty mindset.

The strange thing is, you can have a lot of money and still be trapped by a poverty mindset. You can also have

> Faith-filled **stewardship** is a decision to live **open-handed** before the Lord.

#MindsetMattersBook

very little money and be very generous! The world of the generous gets more substantial and more abundant in every arena of your life, not just in your finances. *Faith-filled stewardship is a decision to live open-handed before the Lord.*

Have you ever been to the beach and picked up a handful of sand? The tighter you squeeze sand, the more of it falls out of your hand. Stinginess is like that, too. The tighter you squeeze, the more you lose in life. But living generously with an open hand allows God to pour more into your hand for you to steward.

Are you living with open or closed hands? Living with an open hand reveals who you trust. Living with a closed grip also reveals who or what you trust. When your hand is open, you can also receive more. It's rather hard to consistently receive something with a closed fist, like trying to catch a football with closed hands. God wants to give you more than what you have now, but only if you can be trusted to make the right choice with more resources.

Generosity is a choice to open your hands and give. There is no manipulation involved, just your free will choosing to be generous. The decision to open your hands in generosity breaks the grip of greed in your life. To put it in faith-terminology, giving breaks a "spirit of mammon" on someone's life.

This is a big reason the church I pastor stopped passing an offering plate during church services. Let me be clear; I don't think it's wrong to pass an offering plate in a worship service. But we live in a high-poverty community. In fact, I'd go as far as to say that there is "spirit of mammon" in our community that keeps people trapped in a poverty mindset, both wealthy and poor alike. It is a mindset motivated by fear. Money has a powerful potential of manipulating hearts, and Christians are not exempt.

As a leadership team, we chose not to pass the offering plate because we didn't want to give any space for a poverty mindset to rule or for people to feel manipulated. Generosity is most powerful when it is an *intentional lifestyle*. We desire to help disciple people into Godly generosity by developing generous hearts over time. We wanted to lead the way in joyful generosity, so we put the offering plates away.

It was a significant shift for all of us as we stepped beyond fear, but God blessed our choice in a big way – beyond what I thought possible! In fact, we saw a significant increase in giving in the first year after making the decision for no more pre-offering mini-sermons and no more passing the plate. Offering boxes and online giving were available, but people would participate because they chose to give.

No compulsion.

No space for misinterpreting motives.

God loves a cheerful giver,[38] and we now have a church who chooses to live with a mindset of joyful generosity!

SPIRIT-FILLED STEWARDSHIP

Stewardship is, in my opinion, showing care or being contentious for something that belongs to someone else. It's an intentional choice for a systematic outcome. Sometimes when we talk about being Spirit-filled or even being Spirit-led, people think that the main indicator of the Holy Spirit's work and leading is spontaneity. It is as if the more unplanned someone's life is, the more guided by the Holy Spirit they are.

As a person who personally believes in the fullness of the Holy Spirit and all His gifts, I call bologna on that idea! Let's be honest, spontaneity isn't even one of the nine fruits of the Spirit. In fact, nowhere in Scripture where the Holy Spirit is being described are terms like "spontaneous" or "reckless" used to describe Him. In fact, the Bible says, *"Many are the plans in a person's heart, but it is the Lord's purpose that prevails."* (Prov. 19:21) There must be a plan for a purpose to be revealed. This verse indicates that God's purposes work with our plans.

Planning is good stewardship. God drops dreams and inspiration into our hearts, but He expects us to start making plans for them to happen. Planning and executing the steps needed to bring something to pass is excellent stewardship of God's dreams and visions. It takes just as much faith to formulate a plan and believe God will do a work, as it does to sit back and wait for it to all come together out of nowhere.

If we're not careful, we will romanticize "spontaneity" in order to justify plain old laziness.

Especially when it comes to the area of our finances, we simply cannot live a life full of faith and be recklessly unplanned at the same time.

THE B-WORD

Budget. How does the word make you feel? I know it may be a curse word for some of you. But, let's reframe that. Having a budget simply means we have planned how to spend our money in advance. The truth is, if we want to have faith-filled stewardship, we simply must live on a budget. That's what faith-filled stewardship is all about. To borrow a phrase from financial guru Dave Ramsey, "Act your wage. Live like no one else, so one day, you can live like no one else."[39]

As a church and organization, we budget each year. We set our expenses 20 percent below what we expect to receive in donations. We give 10 percent to outreach missions and save the other 10 percent. Plus, we are working hard to stay debt-free, even while continually expanding to make room for more people to belong.

These are Biblical principles that we can adopt into our lives; principles that will bring the blessings of God in a new way.

BEYOND MONEY

You see, stewardship is not limited to money. Financial stewardship is the training block for what God really wants us to steward – people.

People are God's most valued commodity and His highest creation on earth. God examines how we handle financial stewardship to see if we can be trusted with the stewardship of people.

Perhaps you are looking to advance in your career and move into management, yet God has not opened a door for you. Is it possible He can't trust you with people yet because He sees how stingy and undisciplined you are with your money?

Think about the "Parable of the Talents" in Scripture.[40] The master in the parable rewards two faithful stewards by making them rulers over cities, expanding their influence over people and communities. But the servant who made financial decisions based on fear, and incorrectly interpreted the master's heart as "stingy," lost everything. Perhaps this is why some people get the opportunity to handle more resources than others. It's not because God likes certain people more, or that He wants to keep other people poor. No, God is waiting to bless and increase all our lives, but He can only expand our influence and wealth at the rate of our character and stewardship can handle it responsibly.

What would it look like for you to set your mind on things of eternal significance? If you had a mindset to live a life of joyful generosity and faith-filled stewardship, what would be different in how you handle your money? Are you ready to start making a shift toward generosity and stewardship? Are you ready to look for practical ways to do that?

PRACTICE MAKES PERMANENT

Here are three ways to begin practicing a mindset of generosity and Biblical stewardship:

1. Tithe

Bring the first 10 percent of your gross income, undesignated, to the local church. I repeat, tithing is the training wheels of generosity. The Bible says we "return the tithe," we don't bring it. Why? Because the tithe belongs to God,[41] we can't give away something that belongs to someone else. God owns it all, you and I just get to steward it.

Remember, generosity is the destination, but tithing is the starting point. You might think, "I don't have enough money to live on already; how can I live off 90 percent when I'm barely making it on 100 percent?" But seeds must be sown before you will ever see a harvest. We all want a harvest of blessing, but seeds must leave our hands, first. Tithing is a choice and returning 10 percent of our increase to God is just returning what belongs to Him, first.

2. Budget

Assign a job to every dollar you make. Tell it where you want it to go and what you want it to do. Make a budget, then adjust it as you need to. Make it your goal to live on less than you earn, so you can start to eliminate debt. FinancialPeaceUniversity.com offers great resources on stewarding your finances in a God-honoring way, if you would like to learn more.

3. Practice Generosity

Even when you don't have a lot of money to give, give little gifts, do random acts of kindness, or leave a bigger tip than usual. Give in other ways besides money, too. For example, make it a habit to regularly give compliments and encouragement to others. Surprise somebody with a thoughtful card or make it a point to smile at everyone. Start practicing generosity little ways like this, and it will eventually become a natural part of your life.

HEALTHY EYESIGHT

I know we've mentioned the verse already in this chapter, but I want to look at the full context of Jesus' words in Matthew 6

> "Do not store up for yourselves treasures on earth, where moths and vermin destroy, and where thieves break in and steal. But store up for yourselves treasures in heaven, where moths and vermin do not destroy, and where thieves do not break in and steal. For where your treasure is, there your heart will be also. "The eye is the lamp of the body. If your

> *eyes are healthy, your whole body will be full of light. But if your eyes are unhealthy, your whole body will be full of darkness. If then the light within you is darkness, how great is that darkness! No one can serve two masters. Either you will hate the one and love the other, or you will be devoted to the one and despise the other. You cannot serve both God and money." (Mt. 6:19-24)*

Jesus tells us in these verses that our eyes are our lamp, and what we fix our eyes upon will eventually flood our lives with light or darkness. In the original language, the reference "healthy eyes" literally refers to a generous life. Conversely, the word "unhealthy eyes" literally refers to being stingy. If we set our attention on dark things like worry, consumerism, and self-indulgences, those things become what we live out and reflect. But if we fix our eyes on God and His ways, light will flood our path!

At the core of a materialistic mindset is this idea of serving Mammon. It is a life driven by fear. "I'm afraid that if I give, I won't have enough. I'm afraid that if I start living on a budget, I won't have any fun and I won't enjoy things. I'm afraid that if I give to God first, everything else is just going to fall apart." We must fight away these fears. We cannot live out God's best if we settle our minds on serving mammon.

Oftentimes, we've allowed our heart to bow down to the wrong thing, and as a result, our eyes became fixed on things or a sort of consumerism that produces dissatisfaction and emptiness within our soul. We must repent and change our thinking.

As you practice these three things – tithing, budgeting, and generosity toward others – you will see God's hand of blessing begin to move in your life. You'll notice an increase on His joy, peace, and provision. I think you will be able to say, like King David, *"I was young and now I am old, yet I have never seen the righteous forsaken or their children begging bread. They are always generous and lend freely; their children will be a blessing."* (Ps. 37:25-26)

Jesus is a much better master than Mammon. When our hearts are bowed to Jesus, rather than Mammon, we can rest from worry. Joyful generosity and faith-filled stewardship will produce God's best in our life!

[9] Final Thoughts

Several years ago, our oldest daughter was getting ready to start school, and I really had been praying for her. It was a new place with new people, and I truly wanted her to be a difference-maker in her world. I was fighting back fearful thoughts of her being around bad influences and not being able to protect her. But I have a personal conviction to raise my kids to face the tough things in life, teaching them to insulate their hearts, rather than isolating them in some Rapunzel-like tower, far away from the real world.

I decided that instead of giving her lots of rules to adhere to, I would help her realize who she was. I would remind her about her identity and her family's identity. I figure if I could help her focus on a few key identity behaviors, she would live out an accurate representation of her character.

And so, as my daughter was getting ready to start kindergarten, there were three things I'd remind her to do every day. I would say, "Sweetheart, we do these three things because we are Hunts. We don't do these things because we're better or different; we do these things because this is who we are and how we've decided to live. We listen to our teachers. We're kind to everyone. We always do our best with a good attitude." Almost daily, I'd remind her of our identity and what we're focusing on, and she'd repeat them back to me.

Now all three of my kids get this daily reminder as I drop them off at school. We also added a fourth one, which is, "We tell the truth." All my kids have these four things memorized and say them every day without help.

These four identity statements are the focus of what we want our kids to embrace and live out. They are the four mindsets, if you will, of the Hunt family. Of course, in the big picture, I want my kids to make an impact in their world. Yes, I want them to have other good habits – good hygiene, get good grades, be productive citizens, and more.

But we must start somewhere. All of this can't be accomplished overnight. So, we drilled it down to four key things that will help lay a solid foundation for so many other essential characteristics.

It has been said that the only way to eat an elephant is one bite at a time.[42] The only way you change the direction of your life is one step at a time. You can make one small choice to move in God's direction. Create one little habit that helps build momentum as you go toward God's best. You can't change everything at once, so just start small. Change a single mindset, first.

Final Thoughts

In this book, we covered seven different mindsets that, as followers of Jesus, will help keep us moving in the right direction. My goal was not to give you an exhaustive list of things to do or rules to keep but to hopefully give you a good grasp on the mindsets that will move you toward experiencing God's best. As you install these mindsets into your mental operating system, you will begin seeing God's character formed in you.

Seven is an intriguing number. Most often, throughout Scripture, the number seven represents completion, finished works, and at times, even divine perfection. While this book is far from divine perfection, these seven mindsets give us a well-rounded approach to walking successfully in God's direction for our lives.

You and I are Christ's ambassadors in this world.[43] We are sons and daughters of a King.[44] Our identity is laced with redemptive potential!

So often, we live below our potential in Christ because we've bought into a lie. For years, that was my story. I was convinced I had something I needed to earn from God, that I was a victim, and that if I didn't perform for others, I wouldn't be accepted.

Each of those lies from the enemy were installed at the very core of my heart. Through life's events, disappointments, and transitions, the enemy was there to whisper and reinforce every one of them. The lies became grooved patterns of thinking that I couldn't seem to stop my

The only way you change the **direction** of your life is **one step at a time.**

#MindsetMattersBook

thoughts from traveling down. These lies became my default operating mode. Scripture refers to these grooved patterns of thought as strongholds birthed from vain imaginations.[45]

One day, by the grace of God, I finally realized that I had bought into a bunch of lies! My mindset needed to be recalibrated to Truth. One by one, I began taking each lie to Jesus, asking Him to give me a Truth to replace it with. I renounced each lie, breaking any agreement I made with it, and then replaced it with God's Truth. I started filtering things through Christ instead of the internal criticism.

You can do the same thing. Here is a sample prayer you can use:

In the name of Jesus, I renounce the lie that (_____). I place it on the cross of Jesus and declare that Jesus has the final word over me. I break every agreement I have with this lie. Jesus, what truth would you like to give me to replace it? (Write down what He tells you.)

Pray that prayer over each lie you know you've believed. As you do, you will sense the peace and presence of the Holy Spirit. Sometimes these lies are so deeply rooted in our core that it takes time to dig them out and remind ourselves of the truth that should be put in their place.

But over time, you will be transformed into a different person. You will be healthier. You will live aligned with God's purposes. Step by step, you can and will move toward the destiny you truly were designed to live. It all starts, though, when you realize that your mindset truly matters, and the good news is that you control your mindset! So set your mind to what matters most!

Endnotes

Chapter [2]

1. Molika Ashford, "How Does a Compass Work?," LiveScience, July 28, 2010. Accessed August 27, 2019. https://www.livescience.com/32732-how-does-a-compass-work.html

2. Nelson, Elizabeth. "Top 5 Branding Mistakes — and Some Hilarious Examples," Upthereeverywhere.com, 2019. Accessed August 27, 2019. https://www.upthereeverywhere.com/blog/top-5-branding-mistakes-and-some-hilarious-examples.

3. 1 Jn. 1:9-10

4. Rom. 12:2

5. 2 Cor. 10:5

6. Jn. 14:6

7. Matt. 28:19

8. 2 Cor. 5:20

9. Rom. 8:16-17

10. Isa. 61:10; Rom. 5:21

Chapter [3]

11. Mk. 10:13

12. Lk. 8:40-56

13. Lk. 19:1-9

14. Jn 4:23,24

Chapter [4]

15. Osgood, Charles. Adapted from "The Responsibility Poem," published on The Osgood File radio broadcast. Accessed December 17, 2019. https://rainbows.typepad.com/blog/2009/10/quote-unquote-charles-osgood-on-responsibility.html

16. Merriam Webster, definition of diligence, (Entry 1 of 2). Accessed December 17, 2019. https://www.merriam-webster.com/dictionary/diligence

17. Matt. 5:16

18. St. Irenaeus, bishop of Lyons. "Man Fully Alive is the Glory of God," Crossroads Initiative. Accessed December 29, 2019. https://www.crossroadsinitiative.com/media/articles/man-fully-alive-is-the-glory-of-god-st-irenaeus/

Chapter [5]

19. Freedman, Liz. "The Developmental Disconnect in Choosing a Major: Why Institutions Should Prohibit Choice until Second Year - The Mentor," Psu.edu, June 28, 2013. Accessed August 27, 2019. https://dus.psu.edu/mentor/2013/06/disconnect-choosing-major/

20. Is. 55:2

21. Is. 55:6-12

22. 2 Cor. 3:18

23. Eph. 2:10

Chapter [6]

24. Ross, Mark. "In Essentials Unity, In Non-Essentials

Liberty, In All Things Charity" Ligonier Ministries, Sept. 1, 2009. Accessed December 27, 2019. https://www.ligonier.org/learn/articles/essentials-unity-non-essentials-liberty-all-things

25. Matt. 16:18

26. Augustine of Hippo quotes, Goodreads.com. Accessed December 23, 2019, https://www.goodreads.com/quotes/110766-if-you-believe-what-you-like-in-the-gospel-and.

Chapter [7]

27. The Merriam-Webster.com Dictionary, s.v. "entitlement (n.)." Accessed December 26, 2019. https://www.merriam-webster.com/dictionary/entitlement.

28. Deut. 8:11,18

29. Is. 55:11, Mk. 4:14-20

30. Jn. 10:10

31. Prov. 18:24

32. 2 Cor. 9:8

33. Eph. 3:20

34. Ps. 136:1-26

35. Ps. 100:4

Chapter [8]

36. Charity Water. 2017. "Birthdays Are Changing the World." Charitywater.Org. Charity Water. 2017. Accessed August 27, 2019. https://archive.charitywater.org/get-involved/pledge-birthday/history/.

37. Eph. 3:20

38. 2 Cor. 9:6-11

39. Ramsey, Dave. Dave Ramsey: quotes, quotable quote ""If you will live like no one else, later you can live like no one else." goodreads.com. Accessed December 28, 2019.
https://www.goodreads.com/quotes/19772-if-you-will-live-like-no-one-else-later-you

40. Luke 19:11-27

41. Mal. 3:8-12

Chapter [9]

42. Cody, Frank. Superintendent of Schools, 1921. Accessed December 29, 2019. https://www.barrypopik.com/index.php/new_york_city/entry/how_do_you_eat_an_elephant

43. 2 Corinthians 5:20

44. Galatians 3:26

45. 2 Cor. 10:3-6

www.ingramcontent.com/pod-product-compliance
Lightning Source LLC
Chambersburg PA
CBHW070049100426
42734CB00040B/2789